STUDIES IN THE
SERMON
ON THE MOUNT

Discovery House Publishers

Books, music, and videos that feed the soul with the Word of God

Box 3566 Grand Rapids, MI 49501

STUDIES IN THE
SERMON
ON THE MOUNT

GOD'S CHARACTER AND
THE BELIEVER'S CONDUCT

OSWALD CHAMBERS

AUTHOR OF **MY UTMOST FOR HIS HIGHEST**

Studies in the Sermon on the Mount
© 1960
Oswald Chambers Publications Association Limited

First published in 1960. Reprinted 1968, 1972, & 1976

This edition copyright © 1995
Oswald Chambers Publications Association Limited

Discovery House Publishers is affiliated with RBC Ministries,
Grand Rapids, Michigan 49512.

Discovery House books are distributed to the trade exclusively by
Barbour Publishing, Uhrichsville, OH 44683.

Unless indicated otherwise, Scripture quotations are from
The New King James Version. Copyright © 1979, 1980, 1982,
Thomas Nelson Publishers, Inc.

Library of Congress Cataloging-in-Publication Data

Chambers, Oswald, 1874–1917.
    Studies in the sermon on the mount : God's character and the
believer's conduct / by Oswald Chambers.
        p.   cm.
    Previously published : London : Marshall Morgan & Scott, 1960.

    ISBN 1-57293-009-8

    1. Sermon on the mount—Devotional use. 2. Christian life.
I. Title.
BT380.C5 1995
226.9'06—dc20   95–46704
                                                             CIP

Printed in the United States of America

05 06 07 08 09 / CHG / 15 14 13 12 11 10 9

CONTENTS

FOREWORD

TO THE FIRST EDITION

I n the Fifth Study the author says—"Jesus tells His disciples to test preachers and teachers by their fruit. There are two tests—one is the fruit in the life of the preacher, and the other is the fruit of the doctrine." It is a genuine joy to be able to apply these touchstones of character and teaching to the life and words of Oswald Chambers. It was the writer's rare privilege to be in the same home with him and to sit under his ministry for a number of months; to see him daily, and to find in him a patient counselor, an exemplary as well as trustworthy teacher, and a Christlike friend. The following words are none too vividly descriptive of this modern prophet-teacher:

Who never sold the truth to serve the hour,
Nor paltered with eternal God for power,
Who let the turbid stream of rumour flow
Thro' either babbling world high or low;
Whose life is work, whose language rife
With rugged maxims hewn from life,
Who never spoke against a foe.

And as to the second test proposed—the fruit of the doctrine— will there be found in all the church of Christ of today one whose records are more weighty with spiritual values? "But," says some simple soul, "I don't understand him." The more is the pity. Leave then the evening newspaper, the book of religious wonder-tales, the high-flown writings watered with adjectives, but empty of thought or power, and read these pages again and again until the truth soaks through to your innermost consciousness. There is about us a flood of profession, but a failure in possession; a torrent of criticism for those who "follow not us," but a trickling rivulet of sound advice to ourselves. To heed the words of our Lord's Sermon on the Mount as interpreted by Oswald Chambers will transform holiness people into holy people, and faithless verbosity into Christian humility. Unto which glorious result God speed the day!

J. F. KNAPP

PUBLISHER'S FOREWORD

These Bible studies on Matthew 5–7 were first given by Oswald Chambers while he served as lecturer at God's Bible School in Cincinnati in 1907. A favorite among all his writings, they serve to enlarge our understanding of Jesus' teaching on what His life in us really means in terms of its outworking in the believer's experience.

For Chambers, the Christian life is authenticated when the indwelling Spirit applies the principles of Christ to the particular circumstances in which the believer is placed. This is doctrine in work clothes, truth become reality, redemption expressed. And, consistent with all of his writings, the author reminds us in these studies that our focus must be on God alone and not on those among whom we live.

We are pleased to release this edition of *Studies in the Sermon on the Mount* as part of "The Oswald Chambers Library" with the hope that its study will fuel the reader's passion to know and love Jesus Christ, the living Word, and further his or her appreciation for the teaching of God's written Word and the application of its truth in all of life.

THE PUBLISHER

ONE

HIS TEACHING AND OUR TRAINING

MATTHEW 5:1–20

In order to understand the Sermon on the Mount, it is necessary to have the mind of its preacher, and this knowledge can be gained by anyone who will receive the Holy Spirit (see Luke 11:13; John 20:22; Acts 19:2). The Holy Spirit alone can expound the teachings of Jesus Christ. The one abiding method of interpretation of the teachings of Jesus is the Spirit of Jesus in the heart of the believer applying His principles to the particular circumstances in which he or she is placed. "Be transformed by the renewing of your mind," says Paul, "that you may prove"—make out—"what is that good and acceptable and perfect will of God" (Romans 12:2).

Beware of placing our Lord as Teacher first instead of Savior. That tendency is prevalent today, and it is a dangerous tendency. We must know Him first as Savior before His teaching can have any meaning for us or before it can have any meaning other than that of an ideal that leads to despair. Fancy coming to men and women with defective lives and defiled hearts and wrong mainsprings, and telling them to be pure in heart! What is the use of giving us an ideal we cannot possibly attain? We are happier without it. If Jesus is a teacher only, then all He can do is to tantalize us by erecting a standard we cannot come anywhere near. But if by being born again from above we know Him first as Savior, we know that He did not come to teach us only: *He came to make us what He teaches we should be.* The Sermon on the Mount is a statement of the life we will live when the Holy Spirit is having His way with us.

The Sermon on the Mount produces despair in the heart of the natural man, and that is the very thing Jesus means it to do, because as soon as we reach the point of despair we are willing to come as paupers to Jesus Christ and receive from Him. "Blessed are the poor in spirit"—that is the first principle of the kingdom. As long as we have a conceited, self-righteous idea that we can do the thing if God will help us, God has to allow us to go on until we break the neck of our ignorance over some obstacle, then we will be willing to come and receive from Him. The bedrock of Jesus Christ's kingdom is poverty, not possession; not decisions for Jesus Christ, but a sense of absolute futility, "I cannot begin to do it." Then, says Jesus, "Blessed are you." That is the entrance, and it takes us a long while to believe we are poor. The knowledge of our own poverty brings us to the moral frontier where Jesus Christ works.

Every mind has two compartments—conscious and subconscious. We say that the things we hear and read slip away from memory; they do not really, they pass into the subconscious mind. It is the work of the Holy Spirit to bring back into the conscious mind the things that are stored in the subconscious. In studying the Bible, never think that because you do not understand it, therefore it is of no use. A truth may be of no use to you just now, but when the circumstances arise in which that truth is needed, the Holy Spirit will bring it back to your remembrance. This accounts for the curious emergence of the statements of Jesus; we say, "I wonder where that word came from?" Jesus said that the Holy Spirit would "bring to your remembrance all things that I said to you" (John 14:26). The point is, will I obey Him when He does bring it to my remembrance? If I discuss the matter with someone else the probability is that I will not obey. "I did not immediately confer with flesh and blood" (Galatians 1:16). Always trust the originality of the Holy Spirit when He brings a word to your remembrance.

Bear in mind the twofold aspect of the mind; there is nothing supernatural or uncanny about it, it is simply the knowledge of how

God has made us. It is foolish therefore to estimate only by what you consciously understand at the time. There may be much of which you do not begin to grasp the meaning, but as you go on storing your mind with Bible truth, the Holy Spirit will bring back to your conscious mind the word you need and will apply it to you in your particular circumstances. These three things always work together— moral intelligence, the spontaneous originality of the Holy Spirit, and the setting of a life lived in communion with God.

DIVINE DISPROPORTION 5:1-12

Our Lord began His discourse by saying, "Blessed are . . . ," and His hearers must have been staggered by what followed. According to Jesus Christ they were to be blessed in each condition that from earliest childhood they had been taught to regard as a curse. Our Lord was speaking to Jews, and they believed that the sign of the blessing of God was material prosperity in every shape and form, and yet Jesus said, Blessed are you for exactly the opposite: "Blessed are the poor in spirit. . . . Blessed are those who mourn."

(a) The Mines of God (vv. 1–10; compare Luke 6:20–26)

The first time we read the Beatitudes they appear to be simple and beautiful and unstartling statements, and they go unobserved into the subconscious mind. We are so used to the sayings of Jesus that they slip over us unheeded; they sound sweet and pious and wonderfully simple, but they are in reality like spiritual torpedoes that burst and explode in the subconscious mind, and when the Holy Spirit brings them back to our conscious minds we realize what startling statements they are. For instance, the Beatitudes seem merely mild and beautiful precepts for unworldly people and of very little use for the stern world in which we live. We soon find, however, that they contain the dynamite of the Holy Spirit; they explode like spiritual mines, when the circumstances of our lives require them to do so, and rip and tear and revolutionize all our conceptions.

The test of discipleship is obedience to the light when these truths are brought to the conscious mind. We do not hunt through the Bible for some precept to obey—Jesus Christ's teaching never leads to making ourselves moral prigs—but we live so in touch with God that the Holy Spirit can continually bring some word of His and apply it to the circumstances we are in. We are not brought to the test until the Holy Spirit brings the word back.

Neither is it a question of applying the Beatitudes literally, but of allowing the life of God to invade us by regeneration, and of then soaking our minds in the teaching of Jesus Christ, which slips down into the subconscious mind. By and by a set of circumstances will arise when one of Jesus Christ's statements emerges, and instantly we have to decide whether we will accept the tremendous spiritual revolution that will be produced if we do obey this precept of His. If we do obey it, our actual lives will become different, and we shall find we have the power to obey if we will. That is the way the Holy Spirit works in the heart of a disciple. The teaching of Jesus Christ comes with astonishing discomfort to begin with, because it is out of all proportion to our natural way of looking at things, but Jesus puts in a new sense of proportion, and slowly we form our way of walking and our conversation on the line of His precepts. Remember that our Lord's teaching applies only to those who are His disciples.

(b) The Motive of Godliness vv. 11–12

The motive at the back of the precepts of the Sermon on the Mount is love of God. Read the Beatitudes with your mind fixed on God, and you will realize their neglected side. Their meaning in relationship to people is so obvious that it scarcely needs stating, but the Godward aspect is not so obvious. "Blessed are the poor in spirit"—toward God. Am I a pauper toward God? Do I know I cannot prevail in prayer; I cannot blot out the sins of the past; I cannot alter my disposition; I cannot lift myself nearer to God? Then I am in the very place where I am able to receive the Holy Spirit. No one can receive the Holy Spirit who is not convinced he or she is a pauper spiritually. "Blessed are the meek"— toward God's dispensations. "Blessed are the merciful"—to God's reputation. Do I awaken sympathy for myself when I am in trouble? Then I am slandering God because the reflex thought in people's minds is, *How hard God is with that individual!* It is easy to slander God's character because He never attempts to vindicate Himself. "Blessed are the pure in heart"—that is obviously Godward. "Blessed are the peacemakers"—between God and humanity, the note that was struck at the birth of Jesus. Is it possible to carry out the Beatitudes? Never! Unless God can do what Jesus Christ says He can, unless He can give us the Holy Spirit who will remake us and bear us into a new realm. The essential element in the life of a saint is simplicity, and Jesus Christ makes the motive of godliness gloriously simple: Be carefully careless about everything except your relationship to Me. The motive of a disciple is to be well pleasing to God. The true blessedness of the saint is in determinedly making and keeping God first. Herein lies the disproportion between Jesus Christ's principles and all other moral teaching: Jesus bases everything on God-realization, while other teachers base everything on self-realization.

There is a difference between devotion to principles and devotion to a person. Jesus Christ never proclaimed a cause; He proclaimed personal devotion to Himself—"for My sake." Discipleship is based not on devotion to abstract ideals, but on devotion to a person, the Lord Jesus Christ; consequently the whole of the Christian life is stamped by originality. Whenever the Holy Spirit sees a chance to glorify Jesus Christ, He will take your whole personality and simply make it blaze and glow with personal passionate devotion to the Lord Jesus. You are no longer devoted to a cause, nor the devotee of a principle; you are the devoted love slave of the Lord Jesus. No one on earth has that love unless the Holy Spirit has imparted it to him or to her. People may admire Him and respect Him and reverence Him, but no one can love God until the Holy Spirit has poured out that love in his or her heart (see Romans 5:5). The only lover of the Lord Jesus Christ is the Holy Spirit.

"Blessed are you when they revile and persecute you, and say all kinds of evil against you falsely for My sake." Jesus Christ puts all the blessedness of high virtue and rare felicity on the ground of— "for My sake." It is not suffering for conscience' sake or for convictions' sake or because of the ordinary troubles of life, but something other than all that—"for My sake."

"Blessed are you when men hate you, and when they exclude you, and revile you, and cast out your name as evil, for the Son of Man's sake." Jesus did not say rejoice when people separate you from their company because of your own crotchety notions—but when they revile you "for My sake." When you begin to deport yourself amongst others as a saint, they will leave you absolutely alone, you will be reviled and persecuted. No one can stand that unless you are in love with Jesus Christ; you cannot do it for a conviction or a creed, but you can do it for a Being whom you love. Devotion to a person is the only thing that tells; devotion to death to a person, not devotion to a creed or a doctrine.

> *Who that one moment has the least descried Him,*
> *Dimly and faintly, hidden and afar,*
> *Doth not despise all excellence beside Him,*
> *Pleasures and powers that are not and that are:—*
>
> *Ay, amid all men bear himself thereafter*
> *Smit with a solemn and a sweet surprise,*
> *Dumb to their scorn and turning on their laughter*
> *Only the dominance of earnest eyes.*

DIVINE DISADVANTAGE vv. 13–16

The disadvantage of a saint in the present order of things is that his or her confession of Jesus Christ is not to be in secret, but glaringly public. It would doubtless be to our advantage from the standpoint of self-realization to keep quiet, and nowadays the tendency to say, "Be a Christian, live a holy life, but don't talk about it," is growing stronger. Our Lord uses in illustration the most conspicuous things—salt, light, and a city set on a hill—and He says, Be like that in your home, in your business, in your church; be conspicuously a Christian for ridicule or respect according to the mood of the people you are with. In Matthew 10:26–28, our Lord taught the need to be conspicuous proclaimers of the truth and not to cover it up for fear of wolfish people.

(a) Concentrated Service v. 13

Not *consecrated* service, but *concentrated*. Consecration would soon be changed into sanctification if we would only concentrate on what God wants. Concentration means pinning down the four corners of the mind until it is settled on what God wants. The literal interpretation of the Sermon on the Mount is child's play; the interpretation by the Holy Spirit is the stern work of a saint, and it requires spiritual concentration.

"You are the salt of the earth." Some modern teachers seem to think our Lord said, You are the sugar of the earth, meaning that gentleness and winsomeness without curativeness is the ideal of the Christian. Our Lord's illustration of a Christian is salt, and salt is the most concentrated thing known. Salt preserves wholesomeness and prevents decay. It is a disadvantage to be salt. Think of the action of salt on a wound, and you will realize this. If you get salt into a wound, it hurts, and when God's children are amongst those who are "raw" towards God, their presence hurts. The person who is wrong with God is like an open wound, and when salt gets in it causes annoyance and distress and the person is spiteful and bitter. The disciples of Jesus in the present dispensation preserve society from corruption; the salt causes excessive irritation, which spells persecution for the saint.

How are we to maintain the healthy, salty tang of saintliness? By remaining rightly related to God through Jesus Christ. In the present dispensation, Jesus says, "The kingdom of God does not come with observation. . . . For indeed, the kingdom of God is within you" (Luke 17:20). People are called on to live out His teaching in an age that will not recognize Him, and that spells limitation and very often persecution. This is the day of the humiliation of the saints; in the next dispensation will be the glorification of the saints, and the kingdom of God will be outside as well as inside people.

(b) Conspicuous Setting vv. 14–16

The illustrations our Lord uses are all conspicuous—salt, light, and a city set on a hill. There is no possibility of mistaking them. Salt, to preserve from corruption, has to be placed in the midst, and before it can do its work it causes excessive irritation, which spells persecution. Light attracts bats and night moths and points out the way for burglars as well as honest people. Jesus would have us remember that society will certainly defraud us. A city is a gathering place for all the human driftwood that will not work for its own living, and a Christian will have any number of parasites and ungrateful hangers-on. All these considerations form a powerful temptation to make us pretend we are not salt, to make us put our light under a bushel and cover our city with a fog, but Jesus will have nothing in the nature of covert discipleship.

"You are the light of the world." Light cannot be soiled; you may try to grasp a beam of light with the sootiest hand, but you leave no mark on the light. A sunbeam may shine into the filthiest hovel in the slums of a city, but it cannot be soiled. A merely moral individual, or an innocent one, may be soiled in spite of his or her integrity; the person who is made pure by the Holy Spirit cannot be soiled but is as light. Thank God for the men and women who are spending their lives in the slums of the earth, not as social reformers to lift their brothers and sisters to cleaner sties, but as the light of God, revealing a way back to God. God keeps them as the light, unsullied. If you have been covering your light, uncover it! Walk as children of light. The light always reveals and guides; people dislike it and prefer darkness when their deeds are evil (John 3:19–20).

Are we the salt of the earth? Are we the light of the world? Are we allowing God to exhibit in our lives the truth of these startling statements of Jesus Christ?

DIVINE DECLARATION vv. 17–20

(a) His Mission vv. 17–19

"I did not come to destroy but to fulfill." An amazing word! Our shoes ought to be off our feet and every commonsense mood stripped from our minds when we hear Jesus Christ speak. In Him we deal with God as human, the God-Man, the representative of the whole human race in one person. The men of His day traced their religious pedigree back to the constitution of God, and this young Nazarene carpenter says, I am the constitution of God; consequently to them He was a blasphemer.

Our Lord places Himself as the exact meaning and fulfillment of all Old Testament prophecies: His mission, He says, is to fulfill the Law and the Prophets, and He further says that anyone who breaks the old laws because they belong to a former dispensation and teaches others to break them shall suffer severe impoverishment. If the old commandments were difficult, our Lord's principles are unfathomably more difficult. Our Lord goes behind the old law to the disposition. Everything He teaches is impossible unless He can put into us His Spirit and remake us from within. The Sermon on the Mount is quite unlike the Ten Commandments in the sense of its being absolutely unworkable unless Jesus Christ can remake us.

There are teachers who argue that the Sermon on the Mount supersedes the Ten Commandments, and that, because "we are not under law but under grace" (Romans 6:15), it does not matter whether we honor our fathers and mothers, whether we covet, and so forth. Beware of statements like this: There is no need nowadays to observe giving the tenth either of money or of time; we are in a new dispensation and everything belongs to God. That, in practical application, is sentimental dust-throwing. The giving of the tenth is not a sign that all belongs to God, but a sign that the tenth belongs to God and the rest is ours, and we are held responsible for what we do with it. To be under grace does not mean that we can do as we like. It is surprising how easily we can juggle ourselves out of Jesus Christ's principles by one or two pious sayings repeated sufficiently often. The only safeguard is to keep personally related to God. The secret of all spiritual understanding is to walk in the light—not the light of our convictions, or of our theories, but the light of God (1 John 1:7).

(b) His Message v. 20

"Unless your righteousness exceeds the righteousness of the scribes and Pharisees, you will by no means enter the kingdom of heaven." Think of the most upright individual you know, the most moral, sterling, religious individual (for example, Nicodemus was a Pharisee, so was Saul of Tarsus—"blameless" according to the law) who has never received the Holy Spirit; Jesus says you must exceed that person in righteousness. You have to be not only as moral as the most moral person you know, but infinitely more—to be so right in your actions, so pure in your motives, that God Almighty can see nothing to blame in you.

Is it too strong to call this a spiritual torpedo? These statements of Jesus are the most revolutionary statements human ears ever listened to, and it needs the Holy Spirit to interpret them to us; the shallow admiration for Jesus Christ as a teacher that is taught today is of no use.

Who is going to climb that "hill of the Lord"? To stand before God and say, "My hands are clean, my heart is pure"—who can do it? Who can stand in the eternal light of God and have nothing for God to blame in him or in her?—only the Son of God; if the Son of God is formed in us by regeneration and sanctification, He will exhibit Himself through our mortal flesh. That is the ideal of Christianity—"that the life of Jesus also may be manifested in our mortal flesh" (2 Corinthians 4:11).

Jesus says our disposition must be right to its depths, not only our conscious motives but our unconscious motives. Now we are beyond our depth. Can God make me pure in heart? Blessed be the name of God, He can! Can He alter my disposition so that when circumstances reveal me to myself, I am amazed? He can. Can He impart His nature to me until it is identically the same as His own? He can. That, and nothing less, is the meaning of His cross and resurrection.

"Unless your righteousness exceeds...." The righteousness of the scribes and Pharisees was right, not wrong; that they did other than righteousness is obvious, but Jesus is speaking here of their righteousness, which His disciples are to exceed. What exceeds right doing if it be not right being? Right being without right doing is possible if we refuse to enter into relationship with God, but that cannot exceed the righteousness of the scribes and Pharisees. Jesus Christ's message here is that our righteousness must exceed the righteousness of the scribes and Pharisees in doing—they were nothing in being—or we shall never enter into the kingdom of heaven. The monks in the Middle Ages refused to take the responsibilities of life, and they shut themselves away from the world; all they wanted was to be and not to do. People today want to do the same thing and they cut themselves off from this and that relationship.

That does not exceed the righteousness of the scribes and Pharisees. If our Lord had meant His disciples to exceed in being only, He would not have used the word "exceed"; He would have said, "Unless your righteousness be otherwise than. . . ." We cannot exceed the righteousness of the most moral person we know on the line of what he or she does, but only on the line of what he or she is.

The teaching of the Sermon on the Mount must produce despair in the natural man; if it does not, it is because he has paid no attention to it. Pay attention to Jesus Christ's teaching and you will soon say, "Who is sufficient for these things?" Blessed are the pure in heart. If Jesus Christ means what He says, where are we in regard to it? "Come to Me," says Jesus.

TWO

ACTUAL AND REAL

MATTHEW 5:21–42

THE ACCOUNT WITH PURITY: 5:21–30

(a) *Disposition and Deeds* (vv. 21–22)
(b) *Temper of Mind and Truth of Manner* (vv. 23–26)
(c) *Lust and License* (vv. 27–28)
(d) *Direction of Discipline* (vv. 29–30)

THE ACCOUNT WITH PRACTICE: 5:31–37

(a) *Speech and Sincerity* (v. 33)
(b) *Irreverent Reverence* (vv. 34–36)
(c) *Integrity* (v. 37)

THE ACCOUNT WITH PERSECUTION: 5:38–42

(a) *Insult* (vv. 38–39)
(b) *Extortion* (v. 40)
(c) *Tyranny* (vv. 41–42)

One cannot take in anything one has not begun to think about; consequently, until a person is born again, what Jesus says does not mean anything to him or to her. The Bible is a universe of revelation facts that have no meaning for us until we are born from above; when we are born again we see in it what we never saw before. We are lifted into the realm where Jesus lives, and we begin to see what He sees (John 3:3).

By *actual* is meant the things we come in contact with by our senses, and by *real,* that which lies behind, that which we cannot get at by our senses (compare 2 Corinthians 4:18). The fanatic sees the real only and ignores the actual; the materialist looks at the actual only and ignores the real. The only sane Being who ever trod this earth was Jesus Christ because in Him the actual and the real were one. Jesus Christ does not stand first in the actual world, He stands first in the real world; that is why the natural man does not bother his head about Him—"the natural man does not receive the things of the Spirit of God, for they are foolishness to him" (1 Corinthians 2:14). When we are born from above we begin to see the actual things in the light of the real. We say that prayer alters things, but prayer does not alter actual things nearly so much as it alters the one who sees the actual things. In the Sermon on the Mount our Lord brings the actual and the real together.

THE ACCOUNT WITH PURITY vv. 21–30

Our Lord in these verses is laying down the principle that if people are going to follow Him and obey His Spirit, they must lay their account with purity. None can make themselves pure by obeying laws. Purity is not a question of doing things rightly, but of the doer on the inside being right. Purity is difficult to define; it is best thought of as a state of heart just like the heart of our Lord Jesus Christ. Purity is not innocence; innocence is the characteristic of a child, and although, profoundly speaking, a child is not pure, yet its innocence presents us with all that we understand by purity. Innocence in a child's life is a beautiful thing, but men and women ought not to be innocent, they ought to be tested and tried and pure. No one is born pure: purity is the outcome of conflict. The pure individual is not the one who has never been tried, but the one who knows what evil is and has overcome it. And so with virtue and morality, no one is born virtuous and moral; we are born unmoral. Morality is always the outcome of conflict, not of necessity. Jesus Christ demands that purity be explicit as well as implicit—that is, my actual conduct, the actual chastity of my bodily life, the actual chastity of my mind, is to be beyond the censure of Almighty God— not beyond the censure of other people, that would produce Pharisaism; I can always deceive others. Jesus Christ has undertaken by the redemption to put in me a heart that is so pure that God can see nothing to censure in it. That is the marvel of the redemption— that Jesus Christ can give me a new heredity, the unsullied heredity of the Holy Spirit, and if it is there, says Jesus, it will work out in actual history.

In Matthew 15, our Lord tells His disciples what the human heart is like—"Out of the heart proceed" (v. 19), and then follows the ugly catalog. We say, "I never felt any of those things in my heart," and we prefer to trust our innocent ignorance rather than Jesus Christ's penetration. Either Jesus Christ must be the supreme authority on the human heart, or He is not worth listening to. If I make conscious innocence the test, I am likely to come to a place where I will find with a shuddering awakening that what Jesus said is true, and I will be appalled at the possibility of evil in me. If I have never been a blackguard, the reason is a mixture of cowardice and the protection of civilized life, but when I am undressed before God I find that Jesus Christ is right in His diagnosis. As long as I remain under the refuge of innocence, I am living in a fool's paradise. There is always a reason to be found in myself when I try to disprove what Jesus says.

Jesus Christ demands that the heart of a disciple be fathomlessly pure, and unless He can give me His disposition, His teaching is tantalizing. If all He came to do was to mock me by telling me to be what I know I never can be, I can afford to ignore Him, but if He can give me His own disposition of holiness, then I begin to see how I can lay my account with purity. Jesus Christ is the sternest and the gentlest of saviors.

The Gospel of God is not that Jesus died for my sins only, but that He gave Himself for me that I might give myself to Him. God cannot accept goodness from me. He can only accept my badness, and He will give me the solid goodness of the Lord Jesus in exchange for it (see 2 Corinthians 5:21).

(a) Disposition and Deeds vv. 21–22

Our Lord is using an illustration that was familiar to the disciples. If a man disregarded the common judgment, he was in danger of being brought into an inner court, and if he was contemptuous with that court, he was in danger of the final judgment. Jesus uses this illustration of the ordinary exercise of judgment to show what the disposition of a disciple must be like—that my motive, the place I cannot get at myself, must be right—the disposition behind the deed, the motive behind the actual occurrence. I may never be angry in deed, but Jesus Christ demands the impossibility of anger in disposition. The motive of my motives, the spring of my dreams, must be so right that right deeds will follow naturally.

In Psalm 139, the psalmist is realizing that he is too big for himself, and he prays, "O Lord, explore me, search me out, and see if there be any way of grief in me, trace out the dreams of my dreams, the motives of my motives, make these right, and lead me in the way everlasting" (vv. 23–24, author's paraphrase). Deliverance from sin is not deliverance from conscious sin only, it is deliverance from sin in God's sight, and He can see down into a region I know nothing about. By the marvelous atonement of Jesus Christ applied to me by the Holy Spirit, God can purify the springs of my unconscious life until the temper of my mind is unblameable in His sight.

Beware of refining away the radical aspect of our Lord's teaching by saying that God puts something in to counteract the wrong disposition—that is a compromise. Jesus never teaches us to curb and suppress the wrong disposition; He gives a totally new disposition, He alters the mainspring of action. Our Lord's teaching can be interpreted only by the new Spirit which He puts in; it can never be taken as a series of rules and regulations.

Someone cannot imitate the disposition of Jesus Christ: it is either there, or it is not. When the Son of God is formed in me, He is formed in my human nature, and I have to put on the new man in accordance with His life and obey Him; then His disposition will work out all the time. We make our characters out of our dispositions. Character is what we make, disposition is what we are born with; when we are born again we are given new dispositions. One must make one's own character, but one cannot make one's disposition; that is a gift. Our natural dispositions are gifted to us by heredity; by regeneration God gives us the disposition of His Son. Jesus Christ is pure to the depths of His motives, and if His disposition can be formed in me, then I begin to see how I can lay my account with purity. "Do not marvel that I said to you, 'You must be born again'" (John 3:7). If I let God alter my heredity, I will become devoted to Him, and Jesus Christ will have gained a disciple. Many of us who call ourselves Christians are not devoted to Jesus Christ.

Our Lord goes behind the old law to the disposition. Everything He says is impossible unless He can put His Spirit into me and remake me from within, then I begin to see how it can be done. When we are born from above, we do not need to pretend to be saints, we cannot help being saints. Am I going to be a spiritually real man or a whitewashed humbug? Am I a pauper in spirit or conceited over my own earnestness? We are so tremendously in earnest that we are blinded by our earnestness and never see that God is more in earnest than we are. Thank God for the absolute poverty of spirit that receives from Him all the time.

There is only one way in which as a disciple you will know that Jesus has altered your disposition, and that is by trying circumstances. When circumstances put you to the test, instead of feeling resentment you experience a most amazing change within, and you say, "Praise God, this is an amazing alteration! I know now that God has altered me, because if that had happened to me before I would have been sour and irritable and sarcastic and spiteful, but now there is a well of sweetness in me that I know never came from myself." The proof that God has altered our dispositions is not that we persuade ourselves He has, but that we prove He has when circumstances put us to the test. The criticism of Christians is not wrong, it is absolutely right. When anyone says he or she is born again, that individual is put under scrutiny, and rightly so. If we are born again of the Holy Spirit and have the life of Jesus in us by means of His Cross, we must show it in the way we walk and talk and transact all our business.

(b) Temper of Mind and Truth of Manner vv. 23–26

Our Lord in these verses uses another illustration familiar in His day. If a man taking a paschal lamb to the priest as an offering, remembered he had leaven in his house, he had to go back and take out the leaven before he brought his offering. We do not carry lambs to sacrifice nowadays, but the spiritual meaning of the illustration is tremendous; it emphasizes the difference between reality and sincerity.

"If you bring your gift to the altar," says Jesus, "and there remember that your brother has something against you, . . . go your way. First be reconciled to your brother, and then come and offer your gift." Jesus does not mention the other person, He says you go. He does not say go halfway, but go. There is no question of your rights.

Talk about practical home-coming truth! This hits us where we live. No one can stand as a humbug before Jesus Christ for one second. The Holy Spirit makes us sensitive to things we never thought of before. Never object to the intense sensitiveness of the Holy Spirit in you when He is educating you down to the scruple, and never discard a conviction. If it is important enough for the Holy Spirit to have brought it to your mind, that is the thing He is detecting.

The test Jesus gives is not the truth of our manner but the temper of our minds. Many of us are wonderfully truthful in manner but our temper of mind is rotten in God's sight. The thing Jesus alters is the temper of mind.

Jesus says, "If you bring your gift to the altar, and there remember"—not, there you rake up something by a morbid sensitiveness (that is where Satan gets hold of embryo Christians and makes them hyperconscientious), but you "there remember that your brother has something against you," inferring that the Holy Spirit brings it to your memory, never check it; say "Yes, Lord, I recognize it" and obey Him at once, however humiliating it may be.

It is impossible to do this unless God has altered your temper of mind; if you are a saint you will find you have no difficulty in doing what otherwise would be an impossible humiliation. The disposition that will not allow the Son of God to rule is the disposition of my claim to my right to myself. That, and not immorality, is the essence of sin: "I will exercise my right to myself in this particular matter." But if my disposition has been altered, I will obey Jesus at all costs.

Watch the thing that makes you snort morally. If you have not had the temper of your mind altered by Jesus Christ, when the Holy

Spirit brings something to your remembrance to be put right you will say, "No, indeed, I am not going to make that up when I was in the right and they were in the wrong; they will say, 'We knew we would make you say you were sorry.'" Unless you are willing to yield your right to yourself on that point absolutely, you need not pray any more, there is a barrier higher than Calvary between you and God. That is the temper of mind in us all until it has been altered. When it has been altered, the other temper of mind is there that makes reconciliation as natural as breathing, and to our astonishment we find we can do what we could not do before. The instant you obey, you find the temper of your mind is real. Jesus Christ makes us real, not merely sincere. The people who are sincere without being real are not hypocrites; they are perfectly earnest and honest and desirous of fulfilling what Jesus wants, but they really cannot do it, the reason being that they have not received the One who makes them real, the Holy Spirit.

Jesus Christ brings people to the practical test. It is not that I say I am pure in heart, but that I prove I am by my deeds; I am sincere not only in manner but in the attitude of my mind. All through the Sermon on the Mount the same truth is brought out. "Unless your righteousness exceeds the righteousness of the scribes and Pharisees." We have to fulfill all the old law and much more, and the only way it can be done is by letting Jesus alter us within and by remembering that everything He tells us to do we can do. The whole point of our Lord's teaching is, Obey Me, and you will find you have a wealth of power within.

(c) Lust and License vv. 27–28

Our Lord goes to the root of the matter every time with no apology. Sordid? Frantically sordid, but sin is frantically sordid, and there is no excuse in false modesty, or in refusing to face the music of the Devil's work in this life. Jesus Christ faced it and He makes us face it too.

Our natural idea of purity is that it means according obedience to certain laws and regulations, but that is apt to be prudery. There is nothing prudish in the Bible. The Bible insists on purity, not prudery. There are bald, shocking statements in the Bible, but from cover to cover the Bible will do nothing in the shape of harm to the pure in heart. It is to the impure in heart that these things are corrupting. If Jesus Christ can make us only prudish, we would be horrified if we had to go and work amongst the moral abominations of heathendom; but with the purity Jesus Christ puts in He can take us where He went Himself and make us capable of facing the vilest moral corruption, unspotted. He will keep us as pure as He is Himself. We are scandalized at social immoralities because our social sense of honor is upset, but are we cut to the heart when we see someone living in pride against God? When the Holy Spirit is at work He puts in new standards of judgment and proportion.

Remember that every religious sentiment that is not carried out on its right level carries with it a secret immorality. That is the way human nature is constituted; whenever you allow an emotion and do not carry it out on its legitimate level, it will react on an illegitimate level. You have no business to harbor an emotion the conclusion of which you see to be wrong. Grip it on the threshold of your mind in a vice of blood and allow it no more way.

God does not give a person a new body when he or she is saved: the body is the same, but the person is given a new disposition. God alters the mainspring; He puts love in the place of lust. What is lust? The impatience of desire—I must have it at once. Love can wait seven years; lust cannot wait two seconds. Esau and his mess of pottage is a picture of lust; Jacob serving for Rachel is a picture of love. In these verses lust is put on the lowest level, but remember that lust runs from the lowest basis of immorality right up to the very height of spiritual life. Jesus Christ penetrates right straight down to the basis of our desires. If ever anyone is going to stand where lust never strikes, it can only be because Jesus has altered his or her disposition; it is impossible unless Jesus Christ can do what He says He can. A disciple has to be free from the degradation of lust, and the marvel of the redemption is that Jesus can free us from it. Jesus Christ's claim is that He can do for us what we cannot do for ourselves. Jesus does not alter our human nature; it does not need altering: He alters the mainspring. The great marvel of the salvation of Jesus is that He alters heredity. License is the rebellion against all law—I will do what I like and care for no one; liberty is the ability to perform the law—there is no independence of God in my makeup.

Do you see how we are growing? The disciples were being taught by Jesus Christ to lay their account with purity. Purity is too deep down for us to get to naturally. The only exhibition of purity is the purity in the heart of our Lord, and that is the purity He implants in us, and He says we will know whether we have that purity by the temper of mind we exhibit when we come up against things that before would have awakened in us lust and self-desire. It is not only a question of possibility on the inside, but of a possibility that shows itself in performance. That is the only test there is—"He who practices righteousness is righteous" (1 John 3:7).

(d) Direction of Discipline vv. 29–30

If God has altered the disposition, where is the need of discipline? And yet in these verses our Lord speaks of very stern discipline, to the parting with the right hand and with the eye. The reason for the need of discipline is that the body has been used by the wrong disposition, and when the new disposition is put in the old physical case is not taken away. It is left there for me to discipline and turn into an obedient servant to the new disposition (see Romans 6:19).

"If your right hand causes you to sin, cut it off and cast it from you; for it is more profitable for you that one of your members perish, than for your whole body to be cast into hell." What does that mean? It means absolute unflinching sternness in dealing with the right things in yourself that are not the best. "The good is the enemy of the best" in everyone. Not the bad, but the good that is not good enough. Your right hand is not a bad thing, it is one of the best things you have, but Jesus says if it causes you to sin in developing your spiritual life and hinders you in following His precepts, cut it off and cast it from you. Jesus Christ spoke rugged truth. He was never ambiguous, and He says it is better to be maimed than damned, better to enter into life lame in human sight and lovely in God's than to be lovely in human sight and lame in God's. It is a maimed life to begin with, such as Jesus describes in these verses; otherwise we may look all right in the sight of other people but be remarkably twisted and wrong in the sight of God.

One of the principles of our Lord's teaching that we are slow to grasp is that the only basis of the spiritual is the sacrifice of the natural. The natural life is neither moral nor immoral. I make it moral or immoral by my ruling disposition. Jesus teaches that the natural life is meant for sacrifice. We can give it as a gift to God, which is the only way to make it spiritual (see Romans 12:1–2). That is where Adam failed: he refused to sacrifice the natural life and make it spiritual by obeying God's voice. Consequently, he sinned the sin of taking his right to himself. Why did God make it necessary for the natural to be sacrificed to the spiritual by me? God did not. God's order was that the natural should be transformed into the spiritual by obedience; it was sin that made it necessary for the natural to be sacrificed, which is a very different thing. If you are going to be spiritual, you must barter the natural, sacrifice it. If you say, "I do not want to sacrifice the natural for the spiritual," then, Jesus says, you must barter the spiritual. It is not a punishment, but an eternal principle.

This line of discipline is the sternest that ever struck humankind. There is nothing more heroic or more grand than the Christian life. Spirituality is not a sweet tendency towards piety in people who have not enough life in them to be bad; spirituality is the possession of the life of God that is masculine in its strength, and He will make spiritual the most corrupt, twisted, sin-stained life if He be obeyed. Chastity is strong and fierce, and the man or woman who is going to be chaste for Jesus Christ's sake has a gloriously sterling job ahead.

When Jesus Christ has altered the disposition, one has to bring the body into harmony with the new disposition, and cause it to exercise the new disposition, and this can only be done by stern discipline, discipline that will mean cutting off a great many things for the sake of one's spiritual life. There are some things that to us are as a right hand and eye, yet we dare not use them, and the world that knows us says, "How absurd you are to cut off that—whatever is wrong in a right hand?" and they will call us fanatics and cranks. If one has never been a crank or a fanatic, it is a pretty sure sign that one has never begun seriously to consider life. In the beginning the Holy Spirit will check us in doing a great many things that may be perfectly right for everyone else but not right for us. No one can decide for another what is to be cut off, and we have no right to use our present limitations to criticize others.

Jesus says we must be prepared to be limited fools in the sight of others in order to further our spiritual characters. If we are willing to give up wrong things only for Jesus Christ, never let us talk about being in love with Him. We say—"Why shouldn't I? There is no harm in it." For pity's sake, go and do it, but remember that the construction of a spiritual character is doomed when we take that line. Anyone will give up wrong things if he or she knows how, but are we prepared to give up the best we have for Jesus Christ? The only right Christians have is the right to give up our rights.

THE ACCOUNT WITH PRACTICE vv. 31–37

Practice means continually doing that which no one sees or knows but us. Habit is the result of practice—by continually doing a thing it becomes second nature. The difference between people is not a difference of personal power, but that some are disciplined and others are not. The difference is not the degree of mental power but the degree of mental discipline. If we have taught ourselves how to think, we will have mental power plus the discipline of having it under control. Beware of impulse. Impulsiveness is the characteristic of a child, but it ought not to be the characteristic of an adult. It means one has not disciplined oneself. Undeterred impulse is undisciplined power.

Every habit is purely mechanical, and whenever we form a habit it makes a material difference in the brain. The material of the brain alters very slowly, but it does alter, and by repeatedly doing a thing a groove is formed in the material of the brain so that it becomes easier to do the thing again, until at last we become unconscious of doing it. When we are regenerated we can reform by the power and the presence of God every habit that is not in accordance with His life. Never form a habit gradually; do it at once, do it sharply and definitely, and never allow a break. We have to learn to form habits according to the dictates of the Spirit of God. The power and the practice must go together. When we fail it is because we have not practiced, we have not brought the mechanical part of our nature into line. If we keep practicing, what we practice becomes our second nature, and in a crisis we will find that not only does God's grace stand by us, but our own nature also. The practicing is ours, not God's, and the crisis reveals whether or not we have been practicing. The reason we fail is not because of the Devil, but because of inattention on our part arising from the fact that we have not disciplined ourselves.

In verses 31–32, Jesus speaks concerning divorce. Marriage and money form the elemental constitution of personal and social life. They are the touchstones of reality, and around these two things the Holy Spirit works all the time. Marriage is one of the mountain peaks on which God's thunder blasts souls to hell, or on which His light transfigures human lives in the eternal heavens. Jesus Christ faces fearlessly the question of sin and wrong, and He teaches us to face it fearlessly also. There is no circumstance so dark and complicated, no life so twisted, that He cannot put it right. The Bible was not written for babes and fools, it was written for men and women who have to face hell's facts in this life, as well as heaven's facts. If Jesus Christ cannot touch those lives that present smooth faces but have hideous tragedy behind them, what is the good of His salvation? But, bless God, He can. He can alter our dispositions, and He can alter the dreams of our dreams until lust no longer dwells in them.

(a) Speech and Sincerity v. 33

Sincerity means that the appearance and the reality are exactly the same. Remember, says Jesus, that you stand before the tribunal of God, not of society; practice the right kind of speech and your Father in heaven will back up all that is true. If you have to back it up yourself, it is of the Evil One. We ought not to have to call on anyone to back up our word; our word ought to be sufficient; whether people believe us or not is a matter of indifference. We all know some whose word is their bond. There is no need for anyone to back up their word; their characters and lives are quite sufficient. Refrain your speech until you can convey the sincerity of your mind through it. Until the Son of God is formed in us we are not sincere, not even honest, but when His life comes into us, He makes us honest with ourselves and generous and kind toward others.

There is a snare in being able to talk about God's truth easily because frequently that is where it ends. If we can express the truth well, the danger is that we do not go on to know more. Most of us can talk piously—we have the practice but not the power. Jesus is saying that our conversation should spring from such a basis of His Spirit in us that everyone who listens is built up by it. Unaffected sincerity always builds up; corrupt communication makes us feel mean and narrow. There are those who never say a bad word, yet their influence is devilish. Don't pay attention to the outside of the platter, pay attention to that which is within the platter. Practice the speech that is in accordance with the life of the Son of God in you, and slowly and surely your speech and your sincerity will be in accord.

(b) Irreverent Reverence vv. 34–36

In our Lord's day the habit was common, as it is today, of backing up ordinary assertions with an appeal to the name of God. Jesus checks that. He says never call on anything in the nature of God to attest what you say. Speak simply and truly, realizing that truth in a human being is the same as truth in God. To call God in as a witness to back up what you say is nearly always a sign that what you are saying is not true. Similarly, if you can find reasons for the truth of what you say, it is proof that what you say is not strictly true; if it were, you would never have to find reasons to prove it. Jesus Christ puts in a truthfulness that never takes knowledge of itself.

Irreverent reverence is something our Lord checks, that is, talking flippantly about those things that ought only to be mentioned with the greatest reverence. I remember an Indian woman who was wonderfully saved. She was an ugly woman, but at the pronouncement of the name of Jesus Christ, her face was transfigured; the whole soul of the woman was in reverent adoration of her Lord and Master.

(c) Integrity v. 37

Integrity means unimpaired purity of heart. God can make our words the exact expression of the disposition He has put in. Jesus taught by example and by precept that no one should stand up for his or her own honor but only for the honor of another. Our Lord was never careful of His own honor; He "made Himself of no reputation" (Philippians 2:7). People called Him a glutton and a

winebibber, a madman, devil-possessed, and He never opened His
mouth; but as soon as they said a word against His Father's honor,
He not only opened His mouth, but He said some terrible things
(see Mark 11:15–18). Jesus Christ by His Spirit alters our standard
of honor, and disciples will never care what people say of us but
will care tremendously what people say of Jesus Christ; we realize
that our Lord's honor, not our own honor, is at stake in our lives.
What is the thing that rouses you? That is an indication of where
you live.

Scandal should be treated as you treat mud on your clothes. If you
try and deal with it while it is wet, you rub the mud into the texture,
but if you leave it till it is dry you can flick it off with a touch—it is
gone without a trace. Leave scandal alone, never touch it.

Let people do what they like with your truth, but never explain
it. Jesus never explained anything; we are always explaining, and
we get into tangles by not leaving things alone. We need to pray
Saint Augustine's prayer, "O Lord, deliver me from this lust of always
vindicating myself." Our Lord never told His disciples when they
made mistakes; they made any number of blunders, but He went
on quietly planting the truth and let mistakes correct themselves.

In the matter of praise, when we are not sure of having done well
we always like to find out what people think; when we are certain
we have done well, we do not care an atom whether folk praise us
or not. It is the same with regard to fear. We all know people who
say they are not afraid, but the very fact that they say it proves they
are. We have to learn to live on the line of integrity all through.

Another truth we do not sufficiently realize is the influence of
what we think over what we say. One may say wonderfully truthful things, but one's thinking is what tells. It is possible to say truthful things in a truthful manner and to tell a lie in thinking. I can
repeat to another what I heard you say, word for word, every detail
scientifically accurate, and yet convey a lie in saying it, because the
temper of my mind is different from the temper of your mind when

you said it. A lie is not an inexactitude of speech; a lie is in the motive. I may be actually truthful and an incarnate liar. It is not the literal words that count but their influence on others.

Suspicion is always of the Devil and is the cause of people saying more than they need say; in that aspect it "is from the evil one." If we submit children to a skeptical atmosphere and call in question all they say, it will instill the habit of backing up what is said: "Well, ask him if you don't believe me." Such a thought would never occur to a child naturally, it only occurs when the child has to talk to suspicious people who continually say, "Now I don't know whether what you are saying is true." The child gets the idea that it does not speak the truth unless someone backs it up. It never occurs to a pure honest heart to back up what it says; it is a wounding insult to be met with suspicion, and that is why from the first a child ought never to be submitted to suspicion.

ACCOUNT WITH PERSECUTION vv. 38–42

(a) Insult vv. 38–39

If a disciple is going to follow Jesus Christ, that disciple must lay his or her account not only with purity and with practice, but also with persecution. The picture our Lord gives is not familiar to us. In the East, a slap on the cheek is the greatest form of insult; its equivalent with us would be spitting in the face. Epictetus, a Roman slave, said that a slave would rather be thrashed to death than flicked on the cheek. Jesus says, "Whoever slaps you on your right cheek, turn the other to him also." The Sermon on the Mount indicates that when we are on Jesus Christ's errands, no time is to be taken in standing up for ourselves. Personal insult will be an occasion in the saint for revealing the incredible sweetness of the Lord Jesus.

The Sermon on the Mount hits where it is meant to hit, and it hits every time. Jesus says whoever slaps you on your right cheek, as My representative, pay no attention, show a disposition equivalent to turning the other cheek also. Either Jesus Christ was mad to say such things, or He was the Son of God. Naturally, if you do not hit back it is because you are a coward; supernaturally, it is the manifestation of the Son of God in you: both have the same appearance outwardly. The hypocrite and the saint are alike in the public eye; the saint exhibits a meekness that is contemptible in the eyes of the world; that is the immense humiliation of being a Christian. Our strength has to be the strength of the Son of God, and "He was crucified in weakness" (2 Corinthians 13:4). Do the impossible, and as soon as you do, you know that God alone has made it possible.

These things apply to a disciple of Jesus and to no one else. The only way to interpret the words of God is to let the Holy Spirit interpret them for us. Jesus said that the Holy Spirit would bring back to our remembrance what He has said, and His counsel is: when you come across personal insult you must not only not resent it, but you must make it an occasion of exhibiting the Son of God.

The secret of a disciple is personal devotion to a personal Lord, and a disciple is open to the same charge as Jesus was—that of inconsistency, but Jesus Christ was never inconsistent to God. There is more than one consistency. There is the consistency of a little child. A child is never the same, always changing and developing, a consistent child. And there is the consistency of a brick wall, a petrified consistency. A Christian is to be consistent only to the life of the Son of God within, not consistent to hard and fast creeds. People pour themselves into creeds, and God Almighty has to blast them out of their prejudices before they become devoted to Jesus Christ. "The expulsive power of a new affection" is what Christianity supplies. The reality of the life of the Son of God in us must show itself in the appearance of our lives.

The miracle of regeneration is necessary before we can live the Sermon on the Mount. The Son of God alone can live it, and if God can form in us the life of the Son of God as He introduced Him into human history, then we can see how we can live it too, and that is

Jesus Christ's message—"Do not marvel that I said to you, 'You must be born again'" (John 3:7; compare Luke 1:35).

(b) Extortion v. 40

Here is another unfamiliar picture to us, but one that had tremendous meaning in our Lord's day. If a man's cloak and coat were taken from him as the result of a lawsuit, he could get back the loan of the coat to sleep in at night. Jesus uses the illustration to point out what we are going to meet with as His disciples. If people extort anything from you while you are in My service, let them have it, but go on with your work. If you are My disciple, says Jesus, you will have no time to stand up for yourself. Never insist on your rights. The Sermon on the Mount is not, Do your duty, but, Do what is not your duty. It is never your duty not to resist evil. That is only possible to the Son of God in you.

(c) Tyranny vv. 41–42

Under the Roman dominance soldiers could compel anyone to be a baggage carrier for a mile. Simon the Cyrenian is a case in point. The Roman soldiers compelled him to be baggage carrier for Jesus Christ. Jesus says, If you are My disciple, you will always go the second mile, you will always do more than your duty. There will be none of this spirit: "Oh well, I can't do any more, they have always misunderstood and misrepresented me." You will go the second mile, not for their sakes, but for Jesus Christ's sake. It would have been a sorry lookout for us if God had not gone the second mile with us. The first thing God requires of a person is to be born from above, then when he or she goes the second mile for others it is the Son of God within who does it. The only right a Christian has is the right not to insist upon his or her rights. Every time I insist upon my rights I hurt the Son of God. I can prevent the Son of God being hurt if I take the blow myself, but if I refuse to take it, it will go back on Him (compare Colossians 1:24).

Verse 42 is an arena for theological acrobats: "Give to him who asks you, and from him who wants to borrow from you do not turn away." That is the statement either of a madman or of God Incarnate. We always say we do not know what Jesus Christ means when we know perfectly well He means something that is a blunt impossibility unless He can remake us and make it possible. Jesus brings us with terrific force straight up against the impossible, and until we get to the place of despair we will never receive from Him the grace that enables us to do the impossible and to manifest His Spirit. These statements of Jesus revolutionize all our conceptions of charity. Much of our modern philanthropy is based on the motive of giving to the poor because they deserve it, or because we are distressed at seeing them poor. Jesus never taught charity from those motives: He said, "Give to him who asks you," not because he deserves it, but because I tell you to. The great motive in all giving is Jesus Christ's command. We can always find a hundred and one reasons for not obeying our Lord's commands, because we will trust our reasoning rather than His reason, and our reason does not take God into calculation. How does civilization argue? "Do these people deserve what I am giving them?" As soon as you talk like that, the Spirit of God says, Who are you? Do you deserve more than other people the blessings you have?

"Give to him who asks you." Why do we always make this mean money? Our Lord makes no mention of money. The blood of most of us seems to run in gold. The reason we make it mean money is because that is where our hearts are. Peter said "Silver and gold I do not have, but what I do have I give you" (Acts 3:6). God grant we may understand that the spring of giving is not impulse nor inclination, but the inspiration of the Holy Spirit. I give because Jesus tells me to.

The way Christians wriggle and twist and compromise over this verse springs from infidelity to the ruling providence of our heavenly Father. We enthrone common sense as God and say, "It is absurd; if I give to every one who asks, every beggar in the place will be at my door." Try it. I have yet to find the person who obeyed Jesus Christ's command who did not realize that God restrains those who beg. If we try to apply these principles of Jesus Christ's literally without the indwelling Spirit, there will be no proof that God is with us, but when we are rightly related to God and are letting the Holy Spirit apply the words to our circumstances, we shall find the restraining hand of God, for if ever God's ruling is seen, it is seen when a disciple obeys Jesus Christ's commands.

THREE

INCARNATE WISDOM AND INDIVIDUAL REASON

MATTHEW 5:43–6:34

47

DIVINE RULE OF LIFE: 5:43–48

(a) *Exhortation (vv. 43–44)*

(b) *Example (v. 45)*

(c) *Expression (vv. 46–48)*

DIVINE REGION OF RELIGION: 6:1–18

(a) *Philanthropy (vv. 1–4)*

(b) *Prayer (vv. 5–15)*

(c) *Penance (vv. 16–18)*

DIVINE REASONING OF MIND: 6:19–24

(a) *Doctrine of Deposit (vv. 19–21)*

(b) *Doctrine of Division (vv. 22–23)*

(c) *Doctrine of Detachment (v. 24)*

DIVINE REASONINGS OF FAITH: 6:25–34

(a) *Careful Carelessness (v. 25)*

(b) *Careful Unreasonableness (vv. 26–29)*

(c) *Careful Infidelity (vv. 30–32)*

(d) *Concentrated Consecration (vv. 33–34)*

We live in two universes: the universe of common sense, in which we come in contact with things by our senses, and the universe of revelation, with which we come in contact by faith. The wisdom of God fits the two universes exactly; the one interprets the other. Jesus Christ is the expression of the wisdom of God. If we take the commonsense universe and discard the revelation of Jesus Christ we make what He says foolishness, because He talks from the universe of revelation all the time. Jesus Christ lived in the revelation world that we do not see, and until we get into His world we do not understand His teaching at all. In Him we find that the universe of revelation and the universe of common sense were made one, and if ever they are to be one in us it can only be by receiving the heredity of Jesus, the Holy Spirit.

In the commonsense universe the faculty required is intellectual curiosity, but when we enter into the domain from which Jesus Christ talks, intellectual curiosity is ruled out and moral obedience takes the absolute place. "If anyone wants to do His will, he shall know. . . ." (John 7:17). If we are going to find out the secrets of the world we live in, we must work at it. God does not encourage laziness. He has given us instruments whereby we are able to explore this universe and we do it entirely by intellectual curiosity; but when we come to the domain that Jesus Christ reveals, no amount of studying or curiosity will avail an atom. Our ordinary commonsense faculties are of no use. We cannot see God or taste God; we can dispute with Him, but we cannot get at Him by our senses at all, and common sense is apt to say there is nothing other than this universe. How are we to get into contact with this other universe to which Jesus Christ belonged and from which He speaks? We come in contact with the revelation facts of God's universe by faith wrought in us by the Spirit of God, then as we develop in understanding, the two universes are slowly made one in us. They never agree outside Jesus Christ. An understanding of redemption is not necessary to salvation any more than an understanding of life is necessary before we can be born into it. Jesus Christ did not come to found religion, nor did He come to found civilization; they were both here before He came. He came to make us spiritually real in every domain. In Jesus Christ there was nothing secular and sacred; it was all real, and He makes His disciples like Himself.

DIVINE RULE OF LIFE vv. 43–48

In these verses our Lord lays down a divine rule that we by His Spirit have to apply to every circumstance and condition of our lives. Our Lord does not make statements that we have to follow literally; if He did we would not grow in grace. In the realm of God it is a spiritual following, and we have to rely upon His Spirit to teach us to apply His statements to the various circumstances in which we find ourselves.

(a) Exhortation vv. 43–44

Our Lord's exhortation here is to be generous in our behavior to all, whether they be good or bad. The marvel of the divine love is that God exhibits His love not only to good people but to bad people. In our Lord's parable of the two sons we can understand the father loving the prodigal son, but he also exhibits his love to the elder brother, to whom we feel a strong antipathy. Beware of walking in the spiritual life according to your natural affinities. We all have natural affinities—some people we like and others we do not; some people we get on well with and others we do not. Never let those likes and dislikes be the rule of your Christian life. "If we walk in the light as He is in the light, we have fellowship with one another" (1 John 1:7), that is, God gives us fellowship with people for whom we have no natural affinity.

(b) Example v. 45

Woven into our Lord's divine rule of life is His reference to our example. Our example is not a good human being, not even a good Christian human being, but God Himself. We do not allow the big surprise of this to lay hold of us sufficiently. Jesus nowhere says, Follow the best example you have, follow Christians, watch those who love Me and follow them; He says, Follow your Father in heaven—that you may be good men and women? That you may be lovable to all society? No, "that you may be sons of your Father in heaven," and that implies a strong family likeness to Jesus Christ. The example of a disciple is God Almighty and no one less; not the best man or the best woman you know, nor the finest saint you ever read about, but God Himself.

"That you may be sons of your Father in heaven." Our Lord's exhortation to us is to love other people as God has loved us. The love of God is not like the love of a father or a mother; it is the love of God. "God demonstrates *His own love* toward us" (Romans 5:8, emphasis mine). The love of God is revealed in that He laid down His life for His enemies, and Jesus tells us to love other people as God has loved us. As disciples of Jesus, we are to identify ourselves with God's interests in other people, to show to other people what God has shown us, and God will give us ample opportunity in our actual lives to prove that we are perfect as our Father in heaven is perfect.

"You have heard that it was said, 'You shall love your neighbor and hate your enemy.' But I say to you, love your enemies." Again I want to emphasize the fact that the teaching of Jesus Christ does not appear at first to be what it is. At first it appears to be beautiful and pious

and lukewarm, but before long it becomes a ripping and tearing torpedo that splits to atoms every preconceived notion a person ever had.
It takes a long time to get the full force of our Lord's statements. "I
say to you, love your enemies"—an easy thing to do when you have
no enemies; an impossible thing when you have. "Bless those who
curse you"—easy when no one is cursing you, but impossible when
someone is. "Do good to those who hate you, and pray for those who
spitefully use you." It seems easy to do all this when we have no enemies, when no one is cursing or persecuting us; but if we have an
enemy who slanders and annoys and systematically vexes us, and we
read Jesus Christ's statement "I say to you, *love your enemies,*" how
are we going to do it? Unless Jesus Christ can remake us within, His
teaching is the biggest mockery human ears ever listened to. Talk
about the Sermon on the Mount being an ideal! Why, it rends one with
despair—the very thing Jesus means it to do—for when we realize that
we cannot love our enemies, we cannot bless those who curse us, we
cannot come anywhere near the standard revealed in the Sermon on
the Mount, then we are in a condition to receive from God the disposition that will enable us to love our enemies, to pray for those who
spitefully use us, to do good to those who hate us.

"I say to you, love your enemies." Jesus does not say, Love everyone. The Bible never speaks vaguely, it always speaks definitely.
People speak about loving humanity, and about loving the heathen;
Jesus says, "Love your enemies." Our Lord does not say, Bless your
enemies; He says, "Love your enemies." He does not say, Love those
who curse you; He says, "Bless those who curse you." "Do good to
those who hate you,"—not bless them. He does not say, Do good
to those who spitefully use you; He says, "Pray for those who spitefully use you." Each one of these commands is stamped with sheer
impossibility to the natural man. If we reverse the order Jesus has
given it can be done with strain, but kept in His order I defy anyone on earth to be able to do it unless he or she has been regenerated by God the Holy Spirit. When you do love your enemies, you

know that God has done a tremendous work in you, and everyone else knows it too.

(c) Expression vv. 46–48

Christian character is not expressed by good doing, but by God-likeness. It is not sufficient to do good, to do the right thing; we must have our goodness stamped by the image and superscription of God. It is supernatural all through. The secret of a Christian's life is that the supernatural is made natural by the grace of God. The way it is worked out in expression is not in having times of communion with God, but in the practical details of life. The proof that we have been regenerated is that when we come in contact with the things that create a buzz, we find to our astonishment that we have a power to keep wonderfully poised in the center of it all, a power we did not have before, a power that is only explained by the Cross of Jesus Christ.

Verse 48 is a reemphasis of verse 20. The perfection of verse 48 refers to the disposition of God in me—"Therefore you shall be perfect, just as your Father in heaven is perfect," not in a future state, but—you shall be perfect, just as your heavenly Father is perfect—if you let Me work that perfection in you. If the Holy Spirit has transformed us within, we will not exhibit good human characteristics, but divine characteristics in our human nature. There is only one type of holiness and that is the holiness of God, and Jesus gives God Almighty as our example. How many of us have measured ourselves by that standard—the standard of a purity of heart in which God can see nothing to blame?

May this divine rule of our Lord's bring us to the bar of the standard of Jesus Christ. His claim is measured by these tremendous statements of His. He can take the vilest piece of broken earthenware, He can take you and me, and can fit us exactly to the expression of the divine life in us. It is not a question of putting the statements of our Lord in front of us and trying to live up to them, but of receiving His Spirit and finding that we can live up to them as He brings them to our remembrance and applies them to our circumstances.

God grant we may have the courageous range of faith that is required. "Therefore you shall be perfect, just as your heavenly Father is perfect"—and people will take knowledge of me that I am a good man? Never! If ever it is recorded of me, "What a good man that is," I have been a betrayer somewhere. If we fix our eyes on our own whiteness we shall soon get dry rot in our spiritual lives. All our righteousness is "like filthy rags" (Isaiah 64:6) unless it is the blazing holiness of Jesus in us uniting us with Him until we see nothing but Jesus first, Jesus second, and Jesus third. Then when people take knowledge of us, they will not say that we are good, that we have a wonderful whiteness, but that Jesus Christ has done something wonderful in us. Always keep at the source of spiritual blessings—Jesus Christ Himself.

Our Lord says, in verse 30, "For it is more profitable for you that one of your members perish, than for your whole body to be cast into hell." He is referring to a *maimed* life. In verse 48 He says, "Therefore you shall be perfect, just as your Father in heaven is perfect." Is our Father in heaven maimed? Has He a right arm cut off, a right eye plucked out?

In verse 48 Jesus completes the picture He began to give in verse 30. Our Lord's statements embrace the whole of the spiritual life from the beginning to the end. In verses 29–30, He pictures a maimed life; in verse 48 He pictures a full-orbed life of holiness. *Holiness* means a perfect balance between my disposition and the laws of God. The maimed life is the characteristic at the beginning, and if we have not had that characteristic it is questionable whether we have ever received the Holy Spirit. What the world calls fanaticism is the entrance into life. We have to begin the life with God as maimed souls; the swing of the pendulum makes us go to the opposite extreme of what we were in the life of the world. We are so afraid of being fanatical; would to God we were as afraid of being inadequate. We should a thousand times rather be fanatical in the beginning than poor inadequate creatures all our lives, limp and useless. May we get to the place where we are willing to cut off the right arm, to pluck out the right eye, to enter into life lame, maimed, having cut off whatever there was need to, however beautiful. And, blessed be the name of God, we shall find that He will bring every life that obeys Him to a full-orbed unity.

Always make allowances for people when they first enter into life; they have to enter on the fanatical line. The danger is lest they stay too long in the stage of fanaticism. When fanaticism steps over the bounds, it becomes spiritual lunacy. In the beginning of the life in grace we have to limit ourselves all round, in right things as well as wrong; but if, when God begins to bring us out of the light of our convictions into the light of the Lord, we prefer to remain true to our convictions, we become spiritual lunatics. Walking in the light of convictions is a necessary stage, but there is a grander, purer, sterner light to walk in, the light of the Lord.

How impatient we are! When we see a life born from above of the Spirit and the necessary limitations and severances and maimings taking place, we will try and do God's work for Him, and God has to rap us sharply over the knuckles and say, Leave that soul in My care. Always allow for the swing of the pendulum in yourself and in others. A pendulum does not swing evenly at first; it begins with a tremendous swing to one extreme and only gets back to the right balance gradually, and that is how the Holy Spirit brings the grace of God to bear upon our lives. "I do not set aside the grace of God," says Paul (Galatians 2:21).

DIVINE REGION OF RELIGION 6:1–18

In chapter 5, our Lord demands that our dispositions be right with Him in our ordinary natural lives lived to others; in chapter 6, He deals with the domain of our lives lived to God before others. The main idea in the region of religion is, Your eyes on God, not on other people.

(a) Philanthropy vv. 1–4

It was inculcated, as it were, into the very blood of the Jew to look after the stranger (see Deuteronomy 15:7–8; Leviticus 19:8, 10), and in our Lord's day the Pharisees made a tremendous show of giving; they gave from a playacting motive, that they might "have glory from men." They would put their money in the boxes in the women's court of the temple with a great clang which sounded like a trumpet. Jesus tells us not to give that way, with the motive to be seen by others, to be known as generous givers, for "Assuredly, I say to you, they have their reward," that is all there is to it. Briefly summed up these verses mean: Have no other motive in giving than to please God. In modern philanthropy we are egged on with other motives—it will do them good; they need the help; they deserve it. Jesus Christ never brings out that aspect in His teaching; He allows no other motive in giving than to please God. In chapter 5, He says, Give because I tell you to, and here, He teaches us not to have mixed motives. It is very penetrating to ask ourselves this question: *What was my motive in doing that kind act?* We will be astounded at how rarely the Holy Spirit gets a chance to fit our motives on to being right with God. We mix our motives with a hundred and one other considerations. Jesus Christ makes it steadily simple—one motive only—your eyes on God. If you are My disciple, you will never give with any other motive than to please God. The characteristic of Jesus in a disciple is much deeper down than doing good things. It is goodness in motive because the disciple has been made good by the supernatural grace of God.

"But when you do a charitable deed, do not let your left hand know what your right hand is doing." That is, do good until it is an unconscious habit of the life and you do not know you are doing it.

You will be covered with confusion when Jesus Christ detects it. "'Lord, when did we see You hungry and feed You?' . . . 'Inasmuch as you did it to one of the least of these My brethren, you did it to Me'" (Matthew 25:37, 40). That is our Lord's magnanimous interpretation of kind acts that people have never allowed themselves to think anything of. Get into the habit of having such a relationship to God that you do good without knowing you do it; then you will no longer trust your own impulse or your own judgment. You will trust only the inspiration of the Spirit of God. The mainspring of your motives will be the Father's heart, not your own; the Father's understanding, not your own. When you are rightly related to God, He will use you as a channel through which His disposition will flow.

(b) Prayer vv. 5–15

Prayer, says Jesus, is to be looked at in the same way as philanthropy—your eyes on God, not on people. Watch your motive before God; have no other motive in prayer than to know Him. The statements of Jesus about prayer, which are so familiar to us, are revolutionary. Call a halt one moment and ask yourself, Why do I pray? What is my motive? Is it because I have a personal secret relationship to God known to no one but me?

The Pharisees were obliged to pray so many times a day, and they took care that they happened to be in the midst of the city when the hour for prayer came; then in an ostentatious manner they would give themselves to prayer. Jesus says, "You shall not be like the hypocrites." Their motive is to be known as praying men, and, "Assuredly . . . they have their reward." Our Lord did not say it was wrong to pray in the corners of the streets, but He did say that the motive to "be seen by men" was wrong. "But you, when you pray, go into your room, and when you have shut your door, pray to your Father who is in the secret place," that is, get a place for prayer where no one imagines that is what you are doing, shut the door and talk to God in secret. It is impossible to live the life of a disciple without definite times of secret prayer. You will find that the place to enter in is in your business, as you walk along the streets, in the ordinary ways of life, when no one dreams you are praying, and the reward comes openly, a revival here, a blessing there. The Scots have a proverb, "Aye keep a bittie to yersel," and as you go on with God you learn more and more to maintain this secret relationship with God in prayer.

When we pray we give God a chance to work in the unconscious realm of the lives of those for whom we pray. When we come into the secret place it is the Holy Spirit's passion for souls that is at work, not our passion, and He can work through us as He likes. Sects produce a passion for souls; the Holy Spirit produces a passion for Christ. The great, dominating passion all through the New Testament is for our Lord Jesus Christ.

Jesus also taught the disciples the prayer of patience. If you are right with God and God delays the manifested answer to your prayer, don't misjudge Him, don't think of Him as an unkind friend or an unnatural father or an unjust judge (see Matthew 7:9–10; Luke 11:5–8; 18:1–6), but keep at it; your prayer will certainly be answered, for "everyone who asks receives" (Matthew 7:8). "Men always ought to pray and not lose heart" (Luke 18:1), not cave in. Your heavenly Father will explain it all one day, Jesus says. He cannot just now because He is developing your character.

In verse 8 Jesus goes to the root of all prayer—"Your Father knows the things you have need of before you ask Him." Common sense says, "Then why ask Him?" Prayer is not getting things from God, that is a most initial stage; prayer is getting into perfect communion with God; I tell Him what I know He knows in order that I may get to know it as He does. Jesus says, Pray because you have a Father, not because it quietens you, and give Him time to answer. If the life of Jesus is formed in me by regeneration and I am drawing my breath in the fear of the Lord, the Son of God will press forward in front of my common sense and change my attitude to things.

Most of us make the blunder of depending upon our own earnestness and not on God at all. It is confidence in Jesus that tells (see 1 John 5:14). All our fuss and earnestness, all our gifts of prayer are not of the slightest use to Jesus Christ. He pays no attention to them. If you have a gift of prayer, may God wither it up until you learn how to get your prayers inspired by God the Holy Spirit. Do we rely on God or on our own earnestness when we pray? God is never impressed by our earnestness; we are not heard because we are in earnest, but on the ground of redemption only. We have "boldness to enter the Holy Place *by the blood of Jesus*" (Hebrews 10:19, emphasis mine) and by no other way.

"Your Father knows the things you have need of before you ask Him." Remember, says Jesus, your Father is keenly and divinely interested in you, and prayer becomes the blather of a child to its father. We are inclined to take everything and everyone seriously except God. Our Lord took nothing and no one seriously but His Father, and He teaches us to be as children before other people but in earnest before our Father in heaven. Notice the essential simplicity of our Lord's teaching all through—right toward God, right toward God.

(c) Penance vv. 16–18

Penance means putting ourselves into a straitjacket for the sake of disciplining spiritual character. Physical sloth will upset spiritual devotion quicker than anything else. If the Devil cannot get at us by enticing to sin, he will get at us by sleeping sickness spiritually— "Now you cannot possibly get up in the morning to pray, you are working hard all day and you cannot give that time to prayer, God does not expect it of you." Jesus says God does expect it of us. Penance means doing a hardship to the body for the sake of developing the spiritual life. Put your life through discipline but do not say a word about it—"Do not appear to men to be fasting." Jeremy Taylor said that men hang out the sign of the Devil to prove there is an angel within; that is, they wear sad countenances and look tremendously severe in order to prove they are holy. Jesus taught His disciples to be hypocrites, "When you fast, . . . wash your face," never allow anyone to imagine you are putting yourself through discipline. If ever we can tell to others the discipline we put ourselves through in order to further our lives with God, from that moment the discipline becomes useless. Our Lord counsels us to have a relationship between us and God that our dearest friends on earth never guess. When you fast, fast to your Father in secret, not before other people. Do not make a cheap martyr of yourself, and never ask for pity. If you are going through a time of discipline, pretend you are not going through it—"Do not appear to men to fast." The Holy Spirit will apply this to each one of us. There are lines of discipline, lines of limitation—physical and mental and spiritual—and the Holy Spirit will say, You must not allow yourself this and that. Ostensible external fasts are of no use; it is the internal fasting that counts. Fasting from food may be difficult for some, but it is child's play compared with fasting for the development of God's purpose in your life. Fasting means concentration. Five minutes heed to what Jesus says and solid concentration on it would bring about transactions with God that would end in sanctification.

"Do not be like the hypocrites, with a sad countenance. For they disfigure their faces that they may appear to men to be fasting." May God destroy forever "the grief that saps the mind," and the luxury of misery and morbid introspection that people indulge in order to develop holiness, and may we bear the shining faces that belong to the sons of God. "They looked to Him and were radiant" (Psalm 34:5).

DIVINE REASONING OF MIND vv. 19–24

It is a fruitful study to find out what the New Testament says about the mind. The Spirit of God comes through the different writers with the one steady insistence to stir up our minds (see, for example, Philippians 2:5; 2 Peter 1:12–13). Satan comes as an angel of light to those Christians only whose hearts are right but whose minds are not stirred up. Our Lord in these verses in Matthew 6 deals with the mind and tells us how we are to think and to reason about things. Unless we learn to think in obedience to the Holy Spirit's teaching, we will drift in our spiritual experience without any thinking at all. The confusion arises when we try to think and to reason things out without the Spirit of God

(a) Doctrine of Deposit vv. 19–21

The Holy Spirit teaches us to fasten our thinking upon God; then when we come to deal with property and money and everything to do with the matters of earth, He reminds us that our real treasure is in heaven. Every effort to persuade myself that my treasure is in heaven is a sure sign that it is not. When my motive has been put right, it will put my thinking right. "Lay up for yourselves treasures in heaven," meaning, have your banking account in heaven, not on earth; lay up your confidence in God, not in your common sense. It is the trial of your faith that makes you wealthy, and it works in this way: every time you venture out on the life of faith, you will come across something in your actual life that seems to contradict absolutely what your faith in God says you should believe. Go through the trial of faith and lay up your confidence in God, not in your common sense, and you will gain so much wealth in your heavenly banking account, and the more you go through the trial of faith the wealthier you will become in the heavenly regions, until you go through difficulties smilingly and people wonder where your wealth of trust comes from. It is a trial of faith all through. The conflict for the Christian is not a conflict with sin, but a conflict over the natural life being turned into the spiritual life. The natural life is not sinful, the disposition that rules the natural life is sinful; when God alters that disposition, we have to turn the natural life into the spiritual by a steady process of obedience to God, and it takes spiritual concentration on God to do it. If you are going to succeed in anything in this world, you must concentrate on it, practice it, and the same is true spiritually. There are many things you will find you cannot do if you are going to be concentrated on God, things that may be perfectly legitimate and right for others, but not for you if you are going to concentrate on God. Never let the narrowness of your conscience condemn the other person. Maintain the personal relationship, and see that you yourself are concentrated on God—not on your convictions or your points of view, but on God. Whenever you are in doubt about a thing, push it to its logical conclusion—"Is this the kind of thing that Jesus Christ is after or the kind of thing Satan is after?" As soon as your decision is made, act on it.

(b) Doctrine of Division vv. 22–23

In verse 22, our Lord is using the eye as the symbol of conscience in an individual who has been put right by the Holy Spirit. A single eye is essential to correct understanding. One idea runs all through our Lord's teaching—right with God, first, second and third. If we are born again of the Holy Spirit we do not persuade ourselves that we are right with God, we are right with Him because we have been put right by the Holy Spirit. Then if we walk in the light as God is in the light, that will keep the eye single, and slowly and surely all our actions begin to be put into the right relationship, and everything becomes full of harmony and simplicity and peace.

No one has a single motive unless he or she has been born from above; we have single ambitions but not single motives. Jesus Christ is the only One with a single motive, and when His Spirit comes in, the first thing He does is to give someone a single motive, a single eye to the glory of God. The one motive of Jesus is to turn people into children of God, and the one motive of disciples is to glorify Jesus Christ.

"If therefore the light that is in you is darkness, how great is that darkness!" Darkness is my point of view, my right to myself; light is God's point of view. Jesus Christ made the line of demarcation between light and darkness very definite; the danger is lest this division gets blurred. "Men loved darkness rather than light, because their deeds were evil," said Jesus (John 3:19).

(c) Doctrine of Detachment v. 24

"You cannot serve God and mammon." A man or woman of the world says we can; with a little subtlety and wisdom and compromise (it is called diplomacy or tact), we can serve both. The Devil's temptation to our Lord to fall down and worship him, that is, to compromise, is repeated over and over again in Christian experience. We have to realize that there is a division as high as heaven and as deep as hell between the Christian and the world. "Whoever therefore wants to be a friend of the world makes himself an enemy of God" (James 4:4).

This doctrine of detachment is a fundamental theme of our Lord's and runs all through His teaching. You cannot be good and bad at the same time; you cannot serve God and make your own out of the service; you cannot make "Honesty is the best policy" a motive, because as soon as you do, you cease to be honest. The riddling the Spirit of God puts one through is the sternest on earth—Why are you a student for the ministry, a missionary, a preacher of the Gospel? There should be one consideration only—to stand right with God, to see that that relationship is the one thing that is never dimmed, then all other things will right themselves. As soon as that relationship is lost sight of, a multitude of motives begin to work and you soon become worn out. Never compromise with the spirit of mammon. When you are right with God, you become contemptible in the eyes of the world. Put into practice any of the teaching of the Sermon on the Mount and you will be treated with amusement at first; then if you persist, the world will get annoyed and will detest you. What will happen, for instance, if you carry out Jesus Christ's teaching in business? Not quite so much success as you bargained for. This is not the age of the glorification of the saints, but the age of their humiliation. Are you prepared to follow Jesus Christ outside the camp, the special camp to which you belong?

"You cannot serve God and mammon." What is *mammon?* It is the system of civilized life that organizes itself without considering God. We have to stand absolutely true to God's line of things. Thank God for everyone who has learned that the dearest friend on earth is a mere shadow compared with Jesus Christ. There must be a dominant, personal, passionate devotion to Him, and only then are all other relationships right (compare Luke 14:26). Jesus Christ is not teaching ordinary integrity, but supernormal integrity, a likeness to our Father in heaven. In the beginning of our spiritual lives we must make allowance for the swing of the pendulum. It is not by accident but by the set purpose of God that in the reaction we go to the opposite extreme of all we were before. God breaks us from the old life violently, not gradually, and only when we are right with Him does He bring us back into the domain of society; we are to be in the world, but not of it. When we become mature in godliness God trusts His own honor to us by placing us where the world, the flesh, and the Devil may try us, knowing that "He who is in you is greater than he who is in the world" (1 John 4:4).

DIVINE REASONINGS OF FAITH vv. 25–34

Faith is our personal confidence in a Being whose character we know, but whose ways we cannot trace by common sense. By the *reasonings* of faith is meant the practical outworking in our lives of implicit, determined confidence in God. Common sense is mathematical; faith is not mathematical, faith works on illogical lines. Jesus Christ places the strongest emphasis on faith and especially on the faith that has been tried. To have faith tests us for all we are worth; we have to stand in the commonsense universe in the midst of things that conflict with our faith, and place our confidence in the God whose character is revealed in Jesus Christ. Jesus Christ's statements reveal that God is a Being of love and justice and truth; the actual happenings in our immediate circumstances seem to prove He is not; are we going to remain true to the revelation that God is good? Are we doing to be true to His honor, whatever may happen in the actual domain? If we are, we shall find that God in His providence makes the two universes, the universe of revelation and the universe of common sense, work together in perfect harmony. Most of us are pagans in a crisis; we think and act like pagans. Only one out of a hundred is daring enough to bank his or her faith in the character of God.

The golden rule for understanding in spiritual matters is not intellect, but obedience. Discernment in the spiritual world is never gained by intellect; in the commonsense world it is. If a person wants scientific knowledge, intellectual curiosity is his or her guide; but if one wants insight into what Jesus Christ teaches, one can only get it by obedience. If things are dark to us spiritually, it is because there is something we will not do. Intellectual darkness comes because of ignorance; spiritual darkness comes because of something I do not intend to obey.

(a) Careful Carelessness v. 25

Jesus does not say, Blessed is the one who does not think about anything—that person is a fool. He says be carefully careless about everything save one thing—your relationship to God. That means we have to be studiously careful that we are careless about how we stand to self-interest, to food, to clothes, for the one reason only: that we are set on minding our relationship to God. Many people are careless about what they eat and drink, and they suffer for it; they are careless about what they put on, and they look as they have no right to look; they are careless over property, and God holds them responsible for it. Jesus is saying that the great care of the life is to put the relationship to God first and everything else second. Our Lord teaches a complete reversal of all our practical, sensible reasonings. Do not make the ruling factor of your life what you shall eat, or what you shall drink, but make zealous concentration on God the one point of your life. The one dominating abandon of the life is concentration on God, consequently every other carelessness is careless in comparison. In Luke 14:26, our Lord lays down the conditions of discipleship, and He says that the first condition is personal, passionate devotion to Him until every other devotion is hatred in comparison.

"Do not worry about your life." As soon as we look at these words of our Lord, we find them the most revolutionary of statements. We argue in exactly the opposite way, even the most spiritual of us—"I must live, I must make so much money, I must be clothed and fed." That is how it begins; the great concern of the life is not God, but how we are going to fit ourselves to live. Jesus Christ says, Reverse the order, get rightly related to Me first, see that you maintain that as the great care of your life, and never put the concentration of your care on the other things. It is a severe discipline to allow the Holy Spirit to bring us into harmony with the teaching of Jesus in these verses.

(b) Careful Unreasonableness vv. 26–29

Jesus declares it to be unreasonable for a disciple to be careful of all that the natural man says we must be careful over. "Look at the birds of the air, for they neither sow nor reap nor gather into barns; yet your heavenly Father feeds them. Are you not of much more value than they? . . . Consider the lilies of the field, how they grow: they neither toil nor spin; and yet I say to you that even Solomon in all his glory was not arrayed like one of these." Jesus does not use the illustrations of the birds and the flowers by accident. He uses them purposely in order to show the utter unreasonableness, from His standpoint, of being so anxious about the means of living. Imagine the sparrows and blackbirds and thrushes worrying about their feathers! Jesus says they do not trouble about themselves at all. The thing that makes them what they are is not their thought for themselves, but the thought of the Father in heaven. A bird is a hard-working little creature, but it does not work for its feathers, it obeys the law of its life and becomes what it is. Jesus Christ's argument is that if we concentrate on the life He gives us, we will be perfectly free for all other things because our Father is watching the inner life. We have to maintain obedience to the Holy Spirit, who is the real principle of our lives, and God will supply the feathers, for are we not "of much more value than they"?

It is useless to mistake careful consideration of circumstances for that which produces character. One cannot produce an inner life by watching the outer all the time. The lily obeys the law of its life in the surroundings in which it is placed, and Jesus says, as a disciple, consider your hidden life with God; pay attention to the source and God will look after the outflow. Imagine a lily hauling itself out of its pot and saying, "I don't think I look exactly right here." The lily's duty is to obey the law of its life where it is placed by the gardener. Watch your life with God, says Jesus, see that it is right and you will grow as the lily. We are all inclined to say, "I would be all right if only I were somewhere else." There is only one way to develop spiritually, and that is by concentrating on God. Don't bother about whether you are growing in grace or whether you are being of use to others, but believe on Jesus and out of you will flow rivers of living water. "Consider the lilies of the field, how they grow"—they simply are. Take the sea and the air, the sun, the stars and the moon—they all are, and what a ministration they exert! So often we mar God's designed influence through us by our self-conscious effort to be consistent and useful. It seems unreasonable to expect us to consider the lilies, yet that is the only way we can grow in grace. Jesus Christ's argument is that the men and women who are concentrated on their Father in heaven are those who are the fittest to do the work of the world. They have no ulterior motive in arranging their circumstances in order to produce fine characters. They know it cannot be done in that way. How are you to grow in the knowledge of God? By remaining where you are and by remembering that your Father knows where you are and the circumstances you are in. Keep concentrated on Him and, spiritually, you will grow, like the lily.

"Which of you by worrying can add one cubit to his stature?" Jesus is speaking from the implicit domain. How many people are born into the world by taking thought? The springs of natural life cannot be got at by the reasoning of common sense, and when you deal with the life of God in your soul, Jesus says remember that your growth in grace does not depend on your watching it, but on your concentration on your Father in heaven.

Notice the difference between the illustrations we use in talking of spiritual growth and the illustrations Jesus uses. We take our illustrations from engineering enterprises, from cars and airplanes, and so forth, things that compel our attention. Jesus Christ took His illustrations from His Father's handiwork, from sparrows and flowers, things that none of us dream of noticing; we are all breathless and passionate and in a hurry. We may think till all is blue, but Jesus says you cannot add one inch to your height in that way. We cannot possibly develop spiritually in any way other than the way He tells us—by concentration on God. Our Lord's counsel to His disciples is be as the lily and the star. When men and women are born from above we are inclined to become moral police officers who unconsciously present ourselves as better than others, as intolerable spiritual prigs. Who are the people who influence us most? Those who buttonhole us, or those who live their lives as the stars in the heaven and the lily in the field, perfectly simple and unaffected? These are the lives that mold us, our mothers and wives and friends who are of that order, and that is the order the Holy Spirit produces. If you want to be of use, get rightly related to Jesus Christ, and He will make you of use unconsciously every moment you live; the condition is believing on Him.

(c) Careful Infidelity vv. 30–32

Suppose Jesus tells you to do something that is an enormous challenge to your common sense. What are you going to do—hang back? If your nerves are in the habit of doing a thing physically, you will do it every time, until you break the habit deliberately. The same is true spiritually. Over and over again you will get up to what Jesus wants and turn back every time when it comes to the point, like a runner balking a hurdle, until you break the habit and abandon it resolutely. Jesus Christ demands of the individual who trusts in Him the same reckless sporting spirit that the natural man exhibits in life. If anyone is going to do anything worthwhile, there are times when he or she has to risk everything on a leap, and in the spiritual world Jesus Christ demands that we risk everything we hold by our common sense and leap into what He says. As soon as we do, we find that what He says fits on as solidly as our common sense.

Following Jesus Christ is a risk absolutely; we must yield right over to Him, and that is where our infidelity comes in. We will not trust what we cannot see, we will not believe what we cannot trace. Then it is all up with our discipleship. The great word of Jesus to His disciples is *abandon*. When God has brought us into the relationship of disciples, we have to venture on His Word, trust entirely to Him, and watch that when He brings us to the venture, we take it.

Jesus sums up commonsense carefulness in someone indwelt by the Spirit of God as infidelity. If, after you have received the Holy Spirit, you try and put other things first instead of God, you will find confusion. The Holy spirit presses through and says, Where does God come in in this new relationship? In this mapped-out holiday? In these new books you are buying? The Holy Spirit always presses that point until we learn to make concentration on God our first consideration. It is not only wrong to worry, it is real infidelity because it means we do not believe God can look after the little practical details of our lives—it is never anything else that worries us. Notice what Jesus said would choke the word He puts in—the Devil? No, the cares of this world. That is how infidelity begins. It is the little foxes that spoil the vines, the little worries always. The great cure for infidelity is obedience to the Spirit of God. Refuse to be swamped by the cares of this world, cut out nonessentials and continually revise your relationship to God and see that you are concentrated absolutely on Him. The one who trusts Jesus Christ in a definite practical way is freer than anyone else to work in the world. Free from fret and worry, we can go with absolute certainty into daily life because the responsibility of our lives is not on ourselves, but on God. If we accept the revelation of Jesus Christ that God is our Father and that we can never think of anything He will forget, worry becomes impossible.

(d) Concentrated Consecration vv. 33–34

"Seek first the kingdom of God and His righteousness, and all these things shall be added to you." Seek first the kingdom of God— but suppose I do, what about this thing and that? Who is going to look after me? I would like to obey God, but don't ask me to take a step in the dark. We enthrone common sense as almighty God and treat Jesus Christ as a spiritual appendage to it. Jesus Christ hits desperately hard at every one of the institutions we bank all our faith on naturally. The sense of property and of insurance is one of the greatest hindrances to development in the spiritual life. You cannot lay up for a rainy day if you are trusting Jesus Christ.

Our Lord teaches that the one great secret of the spiritual life is concentration on God and His purposes. We talk a lot about consecration, but it ends in sentimentalism because there is nothing definite about it. Consecration ought to mean the definite yielding of ourselves over as saved souls to Jesus and concentrating on that. There are things in actual life that lead to perplexity, and we say— I am in a quandary and I don't know which way to take. "Be renewed in the spirit of your mind," says Paul (Ephesians 4:23), concentrate on God, so that you may make out what is His will. Concentration on God is of more value than personal holiness. God can do what He likes with the man or woman who is abandoned to Him. God saves us and sanctifies us, then He expects us to concentrate on Him in every circumstance we are in. "I did not immediately confer with flesh and blood." When in doubt, haul yourself up short and concentrate on God; every time you do, you will find that God will engineer your circumstances and open the way perfectly securely, the condition on your part being that you concentrate on God.

"Seek first the kingdom of God and His righteousness, and all these things shall be added to you." At the bar of common sense Jesus Christ's statements are those of a fool, but bring them to the bar of faith and the Word of God, and you begin to find with awestruck spirit that they are the words of God.

FOUR

CHARACTER AND CONDUCT

MATTHEW 7:1–12

CHRISTIAN CHARACTERISTICS: 7:1–5

(a) The Uncritical Temper (v. 1)
(b) The Undeviating Test (v. 2)
(c) The Undesirable Truth-Teller (vv. 3–5)

CHRISTIAN CONSIDERATENESS: 7:6–11

(a) The Need to Discriminate (v. 6)
(b) The Notion of Divine Control (vv. 7–10)
(c) The Necessity for Discernment (v. 11)

CHRISTIAN COMPREHENSIVENESS: 7:12

(a) The Positive Margin of Righteousness
(b) The Proverbial Maxim of Reasonableness
(c) The Principal Meaning of Revelation

G iving all diligence, add to your faith virtue" (2 Peter 1:5). Peter is writing to those who are the children of God, those who have been born from above, and he says, Add, give diligence, concentrate. *Add* means all that character means. No one is born with character; we make our own. When a person is born from above a new disposition is given to him or to her, but not a new character; neither naturally nor supernaturally are we born with character. Character is what one makes out of one's disposition as it comes in contact with external things. Character cannot be summed up by what one does in spots, but only by what one is in the main trend of one's existence. When we describe people we fix on the exceptional things, but it is the steady trend of a person's life that tells. Character is that which steadily prevails, not something that occasionally manifests itself. Character is made by things done steadily and persistently, not by the exceptional or spasmodic. That is something God mourns over—"your faithfulness is like a morning cloud," He says (Hosea 6:4). In Matthew 7, our Lord is dealing with the need to make character.

CHRISTIAN CHARACTERISTICS 7:1–5

(a) The Uncritical Temper v. 1

"Judge not, that you be not judged." Criticism is part of the ordinary faculty of human beings; we have a sense of humor, a sense of proportion; we see where things are wrong and pull others to bits; but Jesus says, As a disciple, cultivate the uncritical temper.

In the spiritual domain, criticism is love turned sour. In a whole-some spiritual life there is no room for criticism. The critical faculty is an intellectual one, not a moral one. If criticism becomes a habit it will destroy the moral energy of the life and paralyze spiritual force. The only person who can criticize human beings is the Holy Spirit. None of us dare criticize another, because as soon as we do we put ourselves in a superior position to the ones we criticize. Critics must be removed from what they criticize. Before people can criticize a work of art or a piece of music, their information must be complete. They must stand away from what they criticize as superior to it. No one can ever take that attitude to someone else; if we do, we put ourselves in the wrong position and grieve the Holy Spirit. Someone who is continually criticized becomes good for nothing—the effect of criticism knocks all the gumption and power out of a person. Criticism is deadly in its effect because it divides one's powers and prevents one being a force for anything. That is never the work of the Holy Spirit. The Holy Spirit alone is in the true position of a critic. He is able to show what is wrong without wounding and hurting.

The temper of mind that makes us lynx-eyed in seeing where others are wrong does not do them any good because the effect of our criticism is to paralyze their powers, which proves that the criticism was not of the Holy Spirit; we have put ourselves into the position of superiority. Jesus says a disciple can never stand away from another life and criticize it, therefore He advocates an uncritical temper, "Judge not." Beware of anything that puts you in the place of the superior person.

The counsel of Jesus is to abstain from judging. This sounds strange at first because the characteristic of the Holy Spirit in a Christian is to reveal the things that are wrong, but the strangeness is only on the surface. The Holy Spirit does reveal what is wrong in others, but His discernment is never for purposes of criticism but for purposes of intercession. When the Holy Spirit reveals something of the nature of sin and unbelief in others, His purpose is not to make us feel the smug satisfaction of critical spectators—"Well, thank God, I am not like that"—but to make us so lay hold of God for them that God enables them to turn away from the wrong thing. Never ask God for discernment, because discernment increases your responsibility terrifically; you cannot get out of it by talking but only by bearing up the life in intercession before God until God puts the person right. "If anyone sees his brother sinning a sin which does not lead to death, he will ask, and He will give him life for those who commit sin not leading to death" (1 John 5:16). Our Lord allows no room for criticism in the spiritual life, but He does allow room for discernment and discrimination. If we let these search-lights go straight down to the root of our spiritual lives we will see why Jesus says, Don't judge; we won't have time to. Our whole lives are to be lived so in the power of God that He can pour through us the rivers of living water to others. Some of us are so concerned about the outflow that it dries up. We continually ask, "Am I of any use?" Jesus tells us how to be of use: "Believe in Me, and out of you will flow rivers of living water" (John 7:38, author's paraphrase).

"Judge not, that you be not judged." If we let that maxim of our Lord's sink into our hearts we will find how it hauls us up. "Judge not"—why, we are always at it! The average Christian is the most penetratingly critical individual; there is nothing of the likeness of Jesus Christ. A critical temper is a contradiction to all our Lord's teaching. Jesus says of criticism, Apply it to yourself, never to any-one else. "Why do you judge your brother? . . . For we shall all stand before the judgment seat of Christ" (Romans 14:10). When-ever you are in a critical temper, it is impossible to enter into com-munion with God. Criticism makes you hard and vindictive and cruel and leaves you with the flattering unction that you are a supe-rior person. It is impossible to develop the characteristics of a saint and maintain a critical attitude. The first thing the Holy Spirit does is to give us a spring-cleaning, and there is no possibility of pride being left in a person after that. I never met a man or a woman I could despair of after having discerned all that lies in me apart from the grace of God. Stop having a measuring rod for others. Jesus says regarding judging, *Don't;* be uncritical in your temper, because in the spiritual domain you can accomplish nothing by criticism. One of the severest lessons to learn is to leave the cases we do not understand to God. There is always one fact more, in every life, of which we know nothing, therefore Jesus says, "Judge not." We cannot do it. Once and for all, we have to remember always that this is our Lord's rule of conduct.

(b) The Undeviating Test v. 2

"For with what judgment you judge, you will be judged; and with the same measure you use, it will be measured back to you." This statement of our Lord's is not a haphazard guess, it is an eternal law that works from God's throne right down (see Psalm 18:25–26). The measure you use is measured to you again. Jesus speaks of it here in connection with criticism. If you have been shrewd in finding out the defects of others, that will be exactly the measure used against you; people will judge you in the same way. "I am perfectly certain that man has been criticizing me." Well, what have you been doing? Life serves back in the coin you pay; you are paid back, not necessarily by the same person, but the law holds good—"with what judgment you judge, you will be judged." And it is so with regard to good as well as evil. If you have been generous, you will meet with generosity; if you mete out criticism and suspicion to others, that is the way you will be treated. There is a difference between retaliation and retribution. According to our Lord, the basis of life is retribution, but He allows no room for retaliation.

In Romans 2:1, this principle is applied still more definitely—I am guilty myself of what I criticize in another. Every wrong I see in you, God locates in me; every time I judge you, I condemn myself. "Therefore you are inexcusable, O man, whoever you are who judge, for in whatever you judge another you condemn yourself; for you who judge practice the same things." God does not look at the act, He looks at the possibility. We do not believe the statements of the Bible, to begin with. For instance, do we believe that what we criticize in another we are guilty of ourselves? We can always see sin in another because we are sinners. The reason we see hypocrisy and fraud and unreality in others is because they are all in our own hearts. The great danger is lest we call carnal suspicion the conviction of the Holy Spirit. When the Holy Spirit convicts people, He convicts for conversion, that people might be converted and manifest other characteristics. We have no right to put ourselves in the place of the superior person and tell others what we see is wrong; that is the work of the Holy Spirit.

The great characteristic of the saint is humility. We realize to the full that all these sins and others would have been manifested in us but for the grace of God, therefore we have no right to judge. Jesus says, "Judge not," because if you do judge, it will be measured to you again exactly as you have judged. Which of us would dare stand before God and say, "My God, judge me as I have judged other people"? We have judged others as sinners; if God had judged us like that we would be in hell. God judges us through the marvelous atonement of Jesus Christ.

(c) The Undesirable Truth-Teller vv. 3–5

The kind impudence of the average truth-teller is inspired of the Devil when it comes to pointing out the defects of others. The Devil is lynx-eyed over the things he can criticize, and we are all shrewd in pointing out the speck in a brother's eye. It puts us in a superior position; we are finer spiritual characters.

Where do we find that characteristic? In the Lord Jesus? Never! The Holy Spirit works through the saints unbeknown to them. He works through them as light. If this is not understood, you will think the preacher is criticizing you all the time. He is not; it is the Holy Spirit in the preacher discerning the wrong in you.

The last curse in our lives as Christians is the person who becomes a providence to us; this individual is quite certain we cannot do anything without his or her advice, and if we do not heed it, we are sure to go wrong. Jesus Christ ridiculed that notion with terrific power, "Hypocrite! First remove the plank from your own eye, and then you will see clearly to remove the speck from your brother's eye." *Hypocrite,* means literally, "playactor," one whose reality is not in keeping with one's sincerity. A hypocrite is one who plays two parts consciously for his or her own ends. When we find fault with other people we may be quite sincere, and yet Jesus says in reality we are frauds.

We cannot get away from the penetration of Jesus Christ. If I see the speck in my brother's eye, it is because I have a plank in my own. It is a most home-coming statement. If I have let God remove the plank from my own outlook by His mighty grace, I will carry with me the implicit, sunlight confidence that what God has done for me He can easily do for you, because you have only a splinter—I had a log of wood! This is the confidence God's salvation gives us. We are so amazed at the way God has altered us that we can despair of no one; "I know God can undertake for you, you are only a little wrong. I was wrong to the remotest depths of my mind; I was a mean, prejudiced, self-interested, self-seeking person and God has altered me, therefore I can never despair of you or of anyone."

These statements of our Lord's save us from the fearful peril of spiritual conceit, "God, I thank You that I am not like other men" (see Luke 18:9–14), and they also make us realize why such a man as Daniel bowed his head in vicarious humiliation and intercession, "confessing my sin and the sin of my people" (see Daniel 9:3–21). That call comes every now and again to individuals and to nations.

CHRISTIAN CONSIDERATENESS vv. 6-11

Consider how God has dealt with you and then consider that it is for you to do likewise.

(a) The Need to Discriminate v. 6

"Do not give what is holy to the dogs; nor cast your pearls before swine, lest they trample them under their feet, and turn and tear you in pieces." Jesus Christ is inculcating the need to examine carefully what we present in the way of God's truth to others. If we present the pearls of God's revelation to unspiritual people, God says they will trample the pearls under their feet—not trample us under their feet, that would not matter so much—but they will trample the truth of God under their feet. These words are not human words, but the words of Jesus Christ, and the Holy Spirit alone can teach us what they mean. There are some truths that God will not make simple. The only thing God makes plain in the Bible is the way of salvation and sanctification; after that our understanding depends entirely on our walking in the light. Over and over again people water down the Word of God to suit those who are not spiritual, and consequently the Word of God is trampled under the feet of swine. Ask yourself, "Am I in any way flinging God's truth to unspiritual swine?" Be careful, Jesus says, not to give God's holy things to dogs, a symbol of the folk outside. Don't cast your holy things before them, nor give the pearls of God's truth to people who are "swine." Paul mentions the possibility of the pearl of sanctification being dragged in the mire of fornication; it comes through not respecting this mighty caution of our Lord. We have no right to talk about some points in our experience. There are times of fellowship between Christians when these pearls of precious rarity get turned over and looked at, but if we flaunt them without the permission of God for the means of converting people, we will find that what Jesus says is true—that they will trample them under their feet.

Our Lord never tells us to confess anything but Him, "Whoever confesses Me before men" (Matthew 10:32). Testimonies to the world on the subjective line are always wrong, they are for saints, for those who are spiritual and who understand; but our testimony to the world is our Lord Himself. Confess Him: "He saved me, He sanctified me, He put me right with God." It is always easier to be true to our experience than to Jesus Christ. Many people spurn Jesus Christ in any other phase than that of their particular religious ideas. The central truth is not salvation, nor sanctification, nor the Second Coming; the central truth is nothing less than Jesus Christ Himself. "I, if I am lifted up from the earth, will draw all peoples to Myself" (John 12:32). Error always comes in when we take something Jesus Christ does and preach it as the truth. It is part of the truth, but if we take it to be the whole truth we become advocates of an idea instead of a person, the Lord Himself. The characteristic of an idea is that it has the ban of finality. If we are only true to a doctrine of Christianity instead of to Jesus Christ, we drive our ideas home with sledgehammer blows, and the people who listen to us say, "Well, that may be true," but they resent the way it is presented. When we follow Jesus Christ the domineering attitude and the dictatorial attitude go, and concentration on Jesus comes in.

(b) The Notion of Divine Control vv. 7–10

By the simple argument of these verses our Lord urges us to keep our minds filled with the notion of God's control behind everything and to maintain an attitude of perfect trust. Always distinguish between being possessed of the Spirit and forming the mind of Christ. Jesus is laying down rules of conduct for those who have the Spirit. Train your mind with the idea that God is there. If once the mind is trained on that line, when you are in difficulties it is as easy as breathing to remember, "Why, my Father knows all about it!" It is not an effort, it comes naturally. Before, when perplexities were pressing you would go and ask this one and that; now the notion of the Divine control is forming so powerfully in you that you simply go to God about it. We will always know whether the notion is working by the way we act in difficult circumstances. Who is the first one we go to? What is the first thing we do?—the first power we rely on? It is the working out of the principle indicated in Matthew 6:25–34: God is my Father, He loves me, I can never think of anything He will forget, so why should I worry? Keep the notion strong and growing of the control of God behind all things. Nothing happens in any particular unless God's mind is behind it, so we can rest in perfect confidence. There are times when God cannot lift the darkness, but trust Him. Jesus said God will appear at times like an unkind friend, but He is not; He will appear like an unnatural father, but He is not; He will appear like an unjust judge, but He is not. The time will come when everything will be explained. Prayer is not only asking, it is an attitude of heart that produces an atmosphere in which asking is perfectly natural, and Jesus says, "everyone who asks receives."

A person will get from life everything he or she asks for, because one does not ask for that which one's will is not in. If someone asks wealth from life, that person will get wealth—or was playing the fool when asking. "If you abide in Me," says Jesus, "and My words abide in you, you will ask *what you desire,* and it shall be done for you" (John 15:7, emphasis mine). We pray pious blather, our wills are not in it, and then we say God does not answer; we never asked Him for anything. Asking means that our wills are in what we ask.

You say, "But I asked God to turn my life into a garden of the Lord, and there came the plowshare of sorrow, and instead of a garden I have been given a wilderness." God never gives a wrong answer. The garden of your natural life had to be turned into plowed soil before God could turn it into a garden of the Lord. He will put the seed in now. Let God's seasons come over your soul, and before long your life will be a garden of the Lord.

We need to discern that God controls our asking. We bring in what Paul calls "will worship" (see Colossians 2:23 KJV). *Will* is the whole person active; there are terrific forces in the will. People who gain a moral victory by sheer force of will are the most difficult people to deal with afterward. The profound thing in humans is our will, not sin. Will is the essential element in God's creation of human beings; sin is a perverse disposition that entered into humans. At the basis, the human will is one with God; it is covered up with all kinds of desires and motives, and when we preach Jesus Christ, the Holy Spirit excavates down to the basis of the will and the will turns to God every time. We try to attack people's wills; if we lift up Jesus He will push straight to the will. When Jesus talked about prayer He never said, If the human will turns in that direction. He put it with the grand simplicity of a child—*Ask*. We bring in our reasoning faculties and say, "Yes, but. . . ." Jesus says, "If you abide in Me, and My words abide in you, you will ask what you desire, and it shall be done for you."

(c) The Necessity for Discernment v. 11

"If you then, being evil, know how to give good gifts to your children, how much more will your Father who is in heaven give good things to those who ask Him?" But remember that we have to ask things that are in keeping with the God whom Jesus Christ reveals, things in keeping with His domain. God is not a necromancer. He wants to develop the character of a child of God. We can know "the things of a man" by "the spirit of the man which is in him," but "the things of God" can only be spiritually discerned (see 1 Corinthians 2:9–14).

The discernment referred to here is the habitual realization that every good thing we have has been given to us by the sheer sovereign grace of God. Jesus says, Have this reasoning incorporated into you: how much have you deserved? Nothing, everything has been given to us by God. Then may God save us from the mean, accursed, economical notion that we must only help the people who deserve it. One can almost hear the Holy Spirit shout in the heart, Who are you who talk like that? Did *you* deserve the salvation God has given you? Did *you* deserve to be filled with the Holy Spirit? All that is done by the sheer sovereign mercy of God. "Then be like your Father in heaven," says Jesus; "be perfect even as He is perfect" (Matthew 5:48, author's paraphrase). "This is My commandment, that you love one another as I have loved you" (John 15:12). It is not done once and for all; it is a continual, steadfast, growing habit of the life.

Humility and holiness always go together. Whenever hardness and harshness begin to creep into the personal attitude toward another, we may be certain we are swerving from the light. The preaching must be as stern and true as God's Word—never water down God's truth—but when you deal with others never forget that you are a sinner saved by grace, wherever you stand now. If you stand in the fullness of the blessing of God, you stand there by no other right than the sheer sovereign grace of God.

Over and over again we blame God for His neglect of people by our sympathy with them; we may not put it into words but by our attitude we imply that we are filling up what God has forgotten to do. Never allow that idea, never allow it to come into your mind. In all probability the Spirit of God will begin to show us that people are where they are because we have neglected to do what we ought. Today the great craze is socialism, and people are saying that Jesus Christ came as a social reformer. Nonsense! We are the social reformers; Jesus Christ came to alter us, and we try to shirk our responsibility by putting our work on Him. Jesus alters us and puts us right; then these principles of His instantly make us social reformers. They begin to work straightway where we live, in our relationships to our fathers and mothers, to our brothers and sisters, our friends, our employers, or employees. Consider how God has dealt with you, says Jesus, and then consider that you do likewise to others.

CHRISTIAN COMPREHENSIVENESS v. 12

Christian grace comprehends the whole person. "You shall love the LORD your God with all your *heart,* with all your *soul,* with all your *mind,* and with all your *strength"* (Mark 12:30, emphasis mine). Salvation means not only a pure heart, an enlightened mind, a spirit right with God, but that the whole person is comprehended in the manifestation of the marvelous power and grace of God; body, soul, and spirit are brought into fascinating captivity to the Lord Jesus Christ. An incandescent mantle illustrates the meaning. If the mantle is not rightly adjusted only one bit of it glows, but when the mantle is adjusted exactly and the light shines, the whole thing is comprehended in a blaze of light; every bit of our being is to be absorbed until we are aglow with the comprehensive goodness of God. "The fruit of the Spirit is in all goodness, righteousness, and truth" (Ephesians 5:9). Some of us have goodness only in spots.

(a) The Positive Margin of Righteousness

The limit to the manifestation of the grace of God in us is our bodies, and the whole of our bodies. We can understand the need of a pure heart, of a mind rightly adjusted to God, and a spirit indwelt by the Holy Spirit, but what about the body? That is the margin of righteousness in us. We make a divorce between a clear intellectual understanding of truth and its practical outcome. Jesus Christ never made such a divorce; He takes no notice of our fine intellectual conceptions unless their practical outcome is shown in reality.

There is a great snare in the capacity to understand a thing clearly and to exhaust its power by stating it. Overmuch earnestness blinds the life to reality; earnestness becomes our god. We bank on the earnestness and zeal with which things are said and done, and after a while we find that the reality is not there, the power and presence of God are not being manifested, there are relationships at home or in business or in private that show, when the veneer is scratched, that we are not real. To say things well is apt to exhaust the power to do them, so that a man or a woman has often to curb the expression of a thing with the tongue and turn it into action, otherwise the gift of facile utterance may prevent the doing the things he or she says.

(b) The Proverbial Maxim of Reasonableness

"Therefore, whatever you want men to do to you, do also to them." Our Lord's use of this maxim is positive, not negative. Do to others whatever you want them to do to you—a very different thing from not doing to others what you do not want them to do to you. What would we like other people to do to us? Well, says Jesus, do that to them; don't wait for them to do it to you. The Holy Spirit will kindle your imagination to picture many things you would like others to do to you, and this is His way of telling you what to do to them—"I would like people to give me credit for the generous motives I have." Well, give them credit for having generous motives. "I would like people never to pass harsh judgments on me." Well, don't pass harsh judgments on them. "I would like other people to pray for me." Well, pray for them. The measure of our growth in grace is our attitude toward other people. "You shall love your neighbor as yourself," says Jesus. Satan comes in as an angel of light and says, "But you must not think about yourself." The Holy Spirit will make you think about yourself, because that is His way of educating you so that you may be able to deal with others. He makes you picture what you would like other people to do to you, and then He says, Now go and do those things to them. This verse is our Lord's standard for practical ethical conduct. "Whatever you want men to do to you, do also to them." Never look for right in the other person, but never cease to be right yourself. We always look for justice in this world, but there is no such thing as justice. Jesus says, Never look for justice, but never cease to give it. The stamp all through our Lord's teaching is that of the impossible unless He can make us all over again, and that is what He came to do. He came to give people a new heredity to which His teaching applies.

(c) The Principal Meaning of Revelation

Jesus Christ came to make the great laws of God incarnate in human life; that is the miracle of God's grace. We are to be written epistles, "known and read by all men" (2 Corinthians 3:2). There is no allowance whatever in the New Testament for the individual who says he or she is saved by grace but who does not produce the graceful goods. Jesus Christ by His redemption can make our actual lives in keeping with our religious professions. In our study of the Sermon on the Mount it would be like a baptism of light to allow the principles of Jesus Christ to soak right down to our very makeup. His statements are not put up as standards for us to attain; God remakes us, puts His Holy Spirit in us, then the Holy Spirit applies the principles to us and enables us to work them out by His guidance.

FIVE

IDEAS, IDEALS, AND ACTUALITY

MATTHEW 7:13–29

TWO GATES, TWO WAYS: 7:13-14

(a) *All Noble Things Are Difficult*
(b) *My Utmost for His Highest (vv. 13–14)*
(c) *A Stoot Hairt tae a Stae Brae*

TEST YOUR TEACHERS: 7:15-20

(a) *Possibility of Pretense (v. 15)*
(b) *Place of Patience (v. 16)*
(c) *Principle of Performance (vv. 17–18)*
(d) *Power of Publicity (vv. 19–20)*

APPEARANCE AND REALITY: 7:21-23

(a) *Recognition of Men (v. 21)*
(b) *Remedy Mongers (v. 22)*
(c) *Retributive Measures (v. 23)*

THE TWO BUILDERS: 7:24-29

(a) *Spiritual Castles (v. 24)*
(b) *Stern Crisis (v. 25)*
(c) *Supreme Catastrophe (v. 26–27)*
(d) *Scriptural Concentration (vv. 28–29)*

An idea reveals what it does and no more. When you read a book about life, life looks simple, but when you actually face the facts of life you find they do not come into the simple lines laid down in the book. An idea is like a searchlight: it lights up what it does and no more, while daylight reveals a hundred and one facts the searchlight had not taken into account. An idea is apt to have a ban of finality about it; we speak of the tyranny of an idea.

An ideal embodies our highest conceptions, but it contains no moral inspiration. To treat the Sermon on the Mount merely as an ideal is misleading. It is not an ideal; it is a statement of the working out of Jesus Christ's disposition in actuality in the life of anyone. A person grows ashamed of not being able to fulfill his or her ideals, and the more upright one is, the more agonizing is one's conflict; "I won't lower my ideals," the individual says, "although I can never hope to make them actual." No one is so labored as the one who has ideals that he or she cannot carry out. Jesus Christ says to such, "Come to Me . . . and I will give you rest," that is, I will stay you, put something into you that will make the ideal and the actual one. Without Jesus Christ there is an unbridgeable gap between the ideal and the actual; the only way out is a personal relationship to Him. The salvation of God not only saves us from hell, but alters our actual lives.

TWO GATES, TWO WAYS vv. 13–14

Our Lord continually used proverbs and sayings that were familiar to His hearers, but He put an altogether new meaning to them.

Here He uses an allegory that was familiar in His day, and He lifted it by His inspiration to embody His patient warnings.

Always distinguish between warning and threatening. God never threatens; the Devil never warns. A warning is a great arresting statement of God's, inspired by His love and patience. This throws a flood of light on the vivid statements of Jesus Christ, such as those in Matthew 23. Jesus is stating the inexorable consequence, "How can you escape the damnation of hell?" There is no element of personal vindictiveness. Be careful how you picture our Lord when you read His terrible utterances. Read His denunciations with Calvary in your mind. It is the great, patient love of God that gives the warning. "The way of the unfaithful is hard" (Proverbs 13:15). Go behind that statement in your imagination and see the love of God. God is amazingly tender, but the way of the unfaithful cannot be made easy. God has made it difficult to go wrong, especially for His children.

"Enter by the narrow gate." If anyone tries to enter salvation in any other way than Jesus Christ's way, that individual will find it a broad way, but the end is distress. Erasmus said it took the sharp sword of sorrow, difficulties of every description, heartbreaks and disenchantments, to bring him to the place where he saw Jesus Christ as the altogether lovely One, and, he says, "When I got there I found there was no need to have gone the way I went." There is the broad way of reasonable self-realization, but the only way to a personal knowledge of eternal redemption is straight and narrow. Jesus says, "I am the way" (John 14:6).

There is a difference between salvation and discipleship. A man or a woman can be saved by God's grace without becoming a disciple of Jesus Christ. Discipleship means a personal dedication of the life to Jesus Christ. People are "saved, yet so as through fire" (1 Corinthians 3:15), who have not been worth anything to God in their actual lives. "Go therefore and *make disciples*" (Matthew 28:19, emphasis mine), said Jesus. The teaching of the Sermon on the Mount produces despair only in a person who is not born again. If Jesus came to be a teacher only, He had better have stayed away. What is the use of teaching a human being to be what no human being can be—to be continually self-effaced, to do more than one's duty, to be completely disinterested, to be perfectly devoted to God? If all Jesus Christ came to do was to teach us to be that, He is the greatest taunter that ever presented any ideal to the human race. But Jesus Christ came primarily and fundamentally to regenerate us. He came to put into anyone the disposition that ruled His own life, and as soon as that is given to a person, the teaching of Jesus begins to be possible. All the standards our Lord gives are based on His disposition.

Notice the apparent unsatisfactoriness of the answers of Jesus Christ. He never answered a question that sprang from a person's head, because those questions are never original, they always have the captious note about them. The individual with that type of question wants to get the best of it logically. In Luke 13:23–24, a certain devout man asked Jesus a question, "Lord, are there few who are saved?" and Jesus replied, "Strive to enter through the narrow gate," that is, see that your own feet are on the right path. Our Lord's answers seem at first to evade the issue, but He goes underneath the question and solves the real problem. He never answers our shallow questions; He deals with the great unconscious need that makes them arise. When someone asks an original question out of his or her own personal life, Jesus answers every time.

(a) All Noble Things Are Difficult

Our Lord warns that the devout life of a disciple is not a dream, but a decided discipline that calls for the use of all our powers. No amount of determination can give me the new life of God—that is a gift; where the determination comes in is in letting that new life work itself out according to Christ's standard. We are always in danger of confounding what we can do with what we cannot do. We cannot save ourselves or sanctify ourselves or give ourselves the Holy Spirit; only God can do that. Confusion continually occurs when we try to do what God alone can do and try to persuade ourselves that God will do what we alone can do. We imagine that God is going to make us walk in the light; God will not, it is we who must walk in the light. God gives us the power to do it, but we have to see that we use the power. God puts the power and the life into us and fills us with His Spirit, but we have to work it out. "Work out your own salvation," says Paul (Philippians 2:12), not, work for your salvation, but work it out; and as we do, we realize that the noble life of a disciple is gloriously difficult and the difficulty of it rouses us up to overcome, not faint and cave in. It is always necessary to make an effort to be noble. Jesus Christ never shields a disciple from fulfilling all the requirements of a child of God. Things that are worth doing are never easy. On the ground of redemption the life of the Son of God is formed in our human nature; we have to put on the new man in accordance with His life, and that takes time and discipline. Acquire your soul with patience (see Luke 21:19). *Soul* is my personal spirit manifesting itself in my body, the way I reason and think and look at things. Jesus says that I must lose my soul in order to find it.

We deal with the great massive phases of redemption—that God saves by sheer grace through the Atonement—but we are apt to forget that it has to be worked out in practical living amongst human beings. "You are My friends," says Jesus (John 15: 14), therefore lay down your lives for Me—not go through the crisis of death, but lay out your lives deliberately for Me, take time over it. It is a noble life and a difficult life. God works in us to do His will, only we must do the doing; if we start to do what He commands we find we can do it, because we work on the basis of the noble thing God has done for us in redemption.

(b) My Utmost for His Highest vv. 13–14

God demands of us our utmost in working out what He has worked in. We can do nothing toward our redemption, but we must do everything to work it out in actual experience on the basis of regeneration. Salvation is God's "bit"; it is complete, we can add nothing to it, but we have to bend all our powers to work out His salvation. It requires discipline to live the life of a disciple in actual things. "Jesus, knowing . . . that He had come from God and was going to God, . . . took a towel . . . and began to wash the disciples' feet" (John 13:3–5). It took God Incarnate to do the ordinary menial things of life rightly, and it takes the life of God in us to use a towel properly. This is redemption being actually worked out in experience, and we can do it every time because of the marvel of God's grace.

"If you love Me, keep My commandments" (John 14:15). Jesus makes this the test of discipleship. The motto over our side of the gate of life is, All God's commands I can obey. We have to do our utmost as disciples to prove that we appreciate God's utmost for us and never allow "I can't" to creep in. "Oh, I am not a saint, I can't do that." If that thought comes in, we are a disgrace to Jesus Christ. God's salvation is a glad thing, but it is a holy, difficult thing that tests us for all we are worth. Jesus Christ is "bringing many sons to glory" (Hebrews 2:10), and He will not shield us from any of the requirements of sonship. He will say at certain times to the world, the flesh, and the Devil, Do your worst. I know that "He who is in you is greater than he who is in the world" (1 John 4:4). God's grace does not turn out milksops, but men and women with a strong family likeness to Jesus Christ. Thank God He does give us difficult things to do! Our hearts would burst if there were no way to show our gratitude. "I beseech you therefore, brethren," says Paul, "by the mercies of God, that you present your bodies a *living sacrifice*" (Romans 12:1, emphasis mine).

(c) A Stoot Hairt tae a Stae Brae

A stoot hairt tae a stae brae, that is, "a strong heart to a steep hill." The Christian life is a holy life; never substitute the word *happy* for *holy.* We certainly will have happiness, but as a consequence of holiness. Beware of the idea so prevalent today that a Christian must always be happy and bright—"Keep smiling." That is preaching merely the gospel of temperament. If you make the determination to be happy the basis of your Christian life, your happiness will go from you; happiness is not a cause, but an effect that follows without striving after it. Our Lord insists that we keep to one point, our eyes fixed on the narrow gate and the difficult way, which means pure and holy living.

"Take My yoke upon you and learn from Me" (Matthew 11:29). It seems amazingly difficult to put on the yoke of Christ, but as soon as we do put it on, everything becomes easy. In the beginning of the Christian life it seems easier to drift and to say, "I can't," but when we do put on His yoke, we find, blessed be the name of God, that we have chosen the easiest way after all. Happiness and joy attend, but they are not our aim. Our aim is the Lord Jesus Christ, and God showers the hundredfold more on us all the way along.

In order to keep a stout heart to the steep hills of life, watch continually against worry coming in. *"Let not your heart be troubled"* (John 14:1, emphasis mine) is a command, and it means that worrying is sinful. It is not the Devil who switches folk off Christ's way, but the ordinary steep difficulties of daily life, difficulties connected with food and clothing and situations. The "cares of this world . . . choke the word" said our Lord (Mark 4:19). We all have had times when the little worries of life have choked God's Word and blotted out His face from us, enfeebled our spirits, and made us sorry and humiliated before Him, even more so than the times when we have been tempted to sin. There is something in us that makes us face temptation to sin with vigor and earnestness, but it requires the stout heart that God gives to meet the cares of this life. I would not give much for those who had nothing in their lives to make them say, "I wish I was not in the circumstances I am in."

"In the world you will have tribulation; but be of good cheer, I have overcome the world" (John 16:33)—and you will overcome it too, you will win every time if you bank on your relationship to Me. Spiritual grit is what we need.

"Enter by the narrow gate." We can only get to heaven through Jesus Christ and by no other way. We can only get to the Father through Jesus Christ, and we can only get into the life of a saint in the same way.

TEST YOUR TEACHERS vv. 15–20

In these verses Jesus tells His disciples to test preachers and teachers by their fruit. There are two tests—one is the fruit in the life of the preacher, and the other is the fruit of the doctrine. The fruit of a person's own life may be perfectly beautiful, and at the same time he or she may be teaching a doctrine that, if logically worked out, would produce the Devil's fruit in other lives. It is easy to be captivated by a beautiful life and to argue that therefore what that person teaches must be right. Jesus says, Be careful, test the teacher by the fruit. The other side is just as true, a person may be teaching beautiful truths and have magnificent doctrine, while the fruit in his or her own life is rotten. We say that if one lives a beautiful life, one's doctrine must be right; not necessarily so, says Jesus. Then again we say because one teaches the right thing, therefore one's life must be right; not necessarily so, says Jesus. Test the doctrine by its fruit, and test the teacher by his or her fruit. "Therefore if the Son makes you free, you shall be free indeed" (John 8:36), the freedom of the nature will work out.

"You will know them by their fruits." You do not gather the vindictive mood from the Holy Spirit; you do not gather the passionately irritable mood from the patience of God; you do not gather the self-indulgent mood and the lust of the flesh in private life from the Spirit of God. God never allows room for any of these moods.

As we study the Sermon on the Mount we find that we are badgered by the Spirit of God from every standpoint in order to bring us into a simplicity of relationship to Jesus Christ. The standard is that of a child depending upon God.

(a) Possibility of Pretense v. 15

"Beware of false prophets, who come to you in sheep's clothing, but inwardly they are ravenous wolves." Our Lord here is describing dangerous teachers, and He warns us of those who come clothed in right doctrine, but inwardly their spirit is that of Satan.

It is appallingly easy to pretend. If our eyes are off Jesus Christ, pious pretense is sure to follow. First John 1:7 is the essential condition of the life of the saint, "If we walk in the light *as He is in the light*" (emphasis mine), that is, with nothing folded up, nothing to hide. As soon as we depend upon anything other than our relationship to God, the possibility of pretense comes in, pious pretense, not hypocrisy (a hypocrite is one who tries to live a twofold life for his own ends and succeeds), but a desperately sincere effort to be right when we know we are not.

We have to beware of pretense in ourselves. It is an easy business to appear to be what we are not. It is easy to talk and to preach—and to preach our actual life to damnation. It was realizing this that made Paul say, "I discipline my body . . . lest, when I have preached to others, I myself should become disqualified" (1 Corinthians 9:27). The more facile the expression in words, the less likely is the truth to be carried out in life. There is a peril for the preacher that the listener has not: the peril of expressing a thing and letting the expression react in the exhaustion of never doing it. That is where fasting has to be exercised—fasting from eloquence, from fine literary finish, from all that natural culture makes us esteem, if it is going to lead us into a limping walk with God. "This kind can come out by nothing but prayer and fasting" (Mark 9:29). Fasting is much more than doing without food, that is the least part.

It is fasting from everything that manifests self-indulgence. There is a certain mood in us all that delights in frank speaking, but we never intend to do what we say; we are "enchanted but unchanged." The frank individual is the unreliable one, much more so than the subtle, crafty person, because he or she has the power of expressing a thing right out, and there is nothing more to it.

(b) Place of Patience v. 16

"You will know them by their fruits. Do men gather grapes from thornbushes or figs from thistles?" This warning is against overzealousness on the part of heresy-hunters. Our Lord would have us bide our time. Luke 9:53–55 is a case in point. Take heed that you do not allow carnal suspicion to take the place of the discernment of the Spirit. Fruit, and fruit alone, is the test. If you see the fruit in a life showing itself in thistles, Jesus says you will know the wrong root is there, for you do not gather thistles from any root but a thistle root; but remember that it is quite possible in winter time to mistake a rose tree for something else, unless you are expert in judging. So there is a place for patience, and our Lord would have us heed this. Wait for the fruit to manifest itself and do not be guided by your own fancy. It is easy to get alarmed and to persuade ourselves that our particular convictions are the standards of Christ, and to condemn every one to perdition who does not agree with us; we are obliged to do it because our convictions have taken the place of God in us. God's Book never tells us to walk in the light of convictions, but in the light of the Lord.

Always distinguish between those who object to your way of presenting the Gospel and those who object to the Gospel itself. There may be many who object to your way of presenting the truth, but that does not necessarily mean that they object to God making them holy. Make a place for patience. Wait before passing your verdict. "You will know them by their fruits." Wrong teaching produces its fruit just as right teaching does, if it is given time.

(c) Principle of Performance v. 17–18

"Even so, every good tree bears good fruit, but a bad tree bears bad fruit. A good tree cannot bear bad fruit, nor can a bad tree bear good fruit." If we say we are right with God, the world has a perfect right to watch our private lives and see if we are so. If we say we are born again, we are put under scrutiny, and rightly so. If the performance of our lives is to be steadily holy, the principle of our lives must be holy—if we are going to bring forth good fruit, we must have a good root. It is possible for an airplane to imitate a bird, and it is possible for a human being to imitate the fruit of the Spirit. The vital difference is the same in each: there is no principle of life behind. The airplane cannot persist, it can only fly spasmodically; our imitation of the Spirit requires certain conditions that keep us from the public gaze, then we can get on fairly well. Before we can have the right performance in our lives, the inside principle must be right—we must know what it is to be born from above, to be sanctified and filled with the Holy Spirit, then our lives will bring forth the fruit. Fruit is clearly expounded in the Epistles, and it is quite different from the gifts of the Spirit, or from the manifest seal of God on His own Word. It is "the fruit of the Spirit." Fruit bearing is always mentioned as the manifestation of an intimate union with Jesus Christ (John 15:1–5).

(d) Power of Publicity vv. 19–20

"Every tree that does not bear good fruit is cut down and thrown into the fire. Therefore by their fruits you will know them." Jesus Christ makes publicity the test; He lived His own life most publicly (John 18:20). The thing that enraged our Lord's enemies was the public manner in which He did things; His miracles were the public manifestation of His power. Today people are annoyed at public testimony. It is no use saying, "Oh yes, I live a holy life, but I don't say anything about it," for you certainly do not. The two go together. If a thing has its root in the heart of God, it will want to be public, to get out. It must do things in the external and the open, and Jesus not only encouraged this publicity, He insisted upon it. For good or bad, things must be dragged out. "There is nothing covered that will not be revealed, and hidden that will not be known" (Matthew 10:26). It is God's law that people cannot hide what they really are. If they are His disciples it will be publicly portrayed. In Matthew 10, Jesus warned His disciples of what would happen when they publicly testified, but, He said, don't hide your light under a bushel for fear of wolfish people; be careful only that you don't go contrary to your duty and have your soul destroyed in hell, as well as your body. "Be wise as serpents and harmless as doves." Our Lord warns that the one who will not be conspicuous as His disciple will be made to be conspicuous as His enemy. As surely as God is on His throne, the inevitable principle must work: the revealing of what all of us really are.

One of the dangers of the Higher Christian Life movement is this hole-and-corner aspect—secret times alone with God. God drags everything out in the sun. Paul couples sanctification and fornication, meaning that every type of high spiritual emotion that is not worked out on its legitimate level will react on a wrong level. To be in contact with external facts is necessary to health in the natural world, and the same thing is true spiritually. God's spiritual open air is the Bible. The Bible is the universe of revelation facts; if we live there our roots will be healthy and our lives right. It is of no use to say, "I once had an experience"; the point is, where is it now? Pay attention to the source, and out of you will flow rivers of living water. It is possible to be so taken up with conscious experience in religious life that we are of no use at all.

APPEARANCE AND REALITY vv. 21–23

Our Lord makes the test of goodness not only goodness in intention, but the active carrying out of God's will. Beware of confounding appearance and reality, of judging only by external evidence. God honors His Word no matter who preaches it. The people Jesus Christ refers to in verse 21 were instruments, but an instrument is not a servant. A servant is one who has given up the right to self to the God whom he or she proclaims, a witness to Jesus, a satisfaction to Jesus Christ wherever he or she goes. The baptism of the Holy Spirit turns people into the incarnation of what they preach, until the appearance and the reality are one and the same. The test of discipleship as Jesus is dealing with it in this chapter is fruit bearing in godly character, and the disciple is warned not to be blinded by the fact that God honors His Word even when it is preached from the wrong motive (compare Philippians 1:15).

The Holy Spirit is the One who brings the appearance and the reality into one in us; He does in us what Jesus did for us. The mighty redemption of God is made actual in our experience by the living efficacy of the Holy Spirit. The New Testament never asks us to believe the Holy Spirit; it asks us to receive Him. He makes the appearance and the reality one and the same thing. He works in our salvation and we have to work it out, with fear and trembling lest we forget to. Thank God, He does give us the sporting chance, the glorious risk. If we could not disobey God, our obedience would not be worth anything. The sinless-perfection heresy says that when we are saved we cannot sin; that is a devil's lie. When we are saved by God's grace, God puts into us the possibility of not sinning, and our character from that moment is of value to God. Before we were saved we had not the power to obey, but now He has planted in us on the ground of redemption the heredity of the Son of God; we have the power to obey, and consequently the power to disobey. The walk of a disciple is gloriously difficult, but gloriously certain. On the ground of the perfect redemption of Jesus Christ, we find that we can begin now to walk worthily, that is, with balance. "Looking at Jesus *as He walked,* he [John the Baptist] said, 'Behold the Lamb of God!'" (John 1:35, emphasis mine). Walking is the symbol of the ordinary character of someone, no show to keep up, no veneer. "I know that this is a holy man of God, who passes by us regularly" (2 Kings 4:9).

(a) Recognition of Men v. 21

"Not every one who says to Me, 'Lord, Lord,' shall enter the kingdom of heaven, but he who does the will of My Father in heaven." Human nature is fond of labels, but a label may be the counterfeit of confession. It is so easy to be branded with labels, much easier in certain stages to wear a ribbon or a badge than to confess. Jesus never used the word *testify;* He used a much more searching word, *confess*—"Whoever confesses Me before men" (Matthew 10:32). The test of goodness is confession by doing the will of God. If you deny Me before men, says Jesus, I will also deny you before my Father. As soon as we confess, we must have a badge. If we do not put one on, other people will. Our Lord is warning that it is possible to wear the label without having the goods; it is possible for someone to wear the badge of being His disciple when he or she is not. Labels are all right, but if we mistake the label for the goods we get confused. If the disciple is to discern between the person with the label and the person with the goods, that disciple must have the spirit of discernment—the Holy Spirit. We start out with the honest belief that the label and the goods must go together. They should, but Jesus warns that sometimes they get severed, and we find cases where God honors His Word although those who preach it are not living right lives. In judging preachers, He says, judge them by their fruit.

(b) Remedy Mongers v. 22

"Many will say to me in that day, 'Lord, Lord, have we not prophesied in Your name, cast out demons in Your name, and done many wonders in Your name?'" If we are able to cast out devils and to do wonderful works, surely we are the servants of God? Not at all, says

Jesus. Our lives must bear evidence in every detail. Our Lord warns here against those who utilize His words and His ways to remedy the evils of society while they are disloyal to Him. "Have we not prophesied in Your name, cast out demons . . . and done many wonders?"—not one word of confessing Jesus Christ; one thing only, they have preached Him as a remedy. In Luke 10:20, our Lord told the disciples not to rejoice because the devils were subject to them, but to rejoice because they were rightly related to Him. We are brought back to the one point all the time—an unsullied relationship to Jesus Christ in every detail, private and public.

(c) Retributive Measures v. 23

"And then I will declare to them, 'I never knew you; depart from Me, you who practice lawlessness!' " In these solemn words Jesus says He will have to say to some Bible expositors, some prophetic students, some workers of miracles, "Depart from me, ye that work iniquity" (KJV). To "work iniquity" is to twist out of the straight; these people have twisted the ways of God and made them unequal. "I never knew you"—you never had My Spirit, you spoke the truth and God honored it, but you were never *of* the truth. "Depart from Me," the most appallingly isolating and condemning words that could be said to a human soul.

Only as we rely upon and recognize the Holy Spirit do we discern how this warning of our Lord's works. We are perplexed because people preach the right thing and God blesses the preaching, and yet all the time the Spirit warns—No, no, no. Never trust the best man or woman you ever met; trust the Lord Jesus only. "Lean not on your own understanding" (Proverbs 3:5); "Do not put your trust in princes" (Psalm 146:3); put your trust in no one but Jesus Christ. This warning holds good all the way along. Every character will lead away from God if taken as a guide. We are never told to follow in all the footsteps of the saints, but only in so far as they have obeyed God: "I have sent Timothy . . . who will remind you of my ways in

Christ" (1 Corinthians 4:17, emphasis mine). Keep right with God; keep in the light. All our panics—moral, intellectual, and spiritual—come on that line. Whenever we take our eyes off Jesus Christ we get startled: "There is another one gone down; I did think that one would have stood right." Look to Me, says Jesus.

THE TWO BUILDERS vv. 24–29

The emphasis in these verses is laid by our Lord on hearing and doing. He has given us His disposition, and He demands that we live as His disciples. How are we going to do it? By hearing My words and doing them, says Jesus. We hear only what we listen for. Have we listened to what Jesus has to say? Have we paid any attention to finding out what He did say? Most of us do not know what He said. If we have only a smattering of religion, we talk a lot about the Devil, but what hinders us spiritually is not the Devil nearly so much as inattention. We may hear the sayings of Jesus Christ, but our wills are left untouched; we never do them. The understanding of the Bible only comes from the indwelling of the Holy Spirit making the universe of the Bible real to us.

(a) Spiritual Castles v. 24

We speak of building castles in the air; that is where a castle should be—whoever heard of a castle underground! The problem is how to get the foundation under your castle in the air so that it can stand upon the earth. The way to put foundations under our castles is by paying attention to the words of Jesus Christ. We may read and listen and not make much of it at the time, but by and by we come into circumstances when the Holy Spirit will bring back to us what Jesus said—are we going to obey? Jesus says that the way to put foundations under spiritual castles is by hearing and doing "these sayings of Mine." Pay attention to His words, and give time to doing it. Try five minutes a day with your Bible. The thing that influences us most is not the thing we give most time to, but the thing that springs from our own personal relationship; that is the prime motive that dominates us.

"You call Me Teacher and Lord, and you say well, for so I am"—but is He? Think of the way we back out of what He says! "I have given you an example, that you should do as I have done to you" (John 13:13, 15). We say it is all very well up to a certain point, and then we abandon it. If we do obey the words of Jesus Christ we are sure to be called fanatics. The New Testament associates shame with the gospel (see Romans 1:16; 1 Peter 4:12–13).

(b) Stern Crisis v. 25

Our spiritual castles must be conspicuous, and the test of a building is not its fair beauty but its foundations. There are beautiful spiritual fabrics raised in the shape of books and of lives, full of the finest diction and activities, but when the test comes, down they go. They have not been built on the sayings of Jesus Christ, but built altogether in the air with no foundations under them.

Build up your character bit by bit by attention to My words, says Jesus, then when the supreme crisis comes, you will stand like a rock. The crisis does not come always, but when it does come, it is all up in about two seconds; there is no possibility of pretense, you are unearthed immediately. If you have built yourself up in private by listening to the words of Jesus and obeying them, when the crisis comes it is not your strength of will that keeps you, but the tremendous power of God—"kept by the power of God" (1 Peter 1:5). Go on building yourself up in the Word of God when no one is watching you, and when the crisis comes you will find you will stand like a rock; but if you have not been building yourself up on the Word of God, you will go down, however strong your will. All you build will end in disaster unless it is built on the sayings of Jesus Christ; but if you are doing what Jesus told you to do, nourishing your soul on His Word, you need not fear the crisis, whatever it is.

(c) Supreme Catastrophe vv. 26–27

Every spiritual castle will be tested by a threefold storm: rain, floods, and winds—the world, the flesh, and the Devil—and it will only stand if it is founded on the sayings of Jesus. Every spiritual fabric that is built with the sayings of Jesus, instead of being founded on them, Jesus calls the building of a foolish man. There is a tendency in all of us to appreciate the sayings of Jesus Christ with our intellects, while we refuse to do them; then everything we build will go by the board when the test comes. Paul applies this in 1 Corinthians 3:12–13, "Now if anyone builds on this foundation with gold, silver, precious stones, wood, hay, straw, each one's work shall become clear; for the Day will declare it, because it will be revealed by fire; and the fire will test each one's work, of what sort it is." All has to be tested by the supreme test.

All that we build will be tested supremely, and it will tumble in a fearful disaster unless it is built on the sayings of Jesus Christ. It is easy to build with the sayings of Jesus, to sling texts of Scripture together and build them into any kind of fabric. But Jesus brings the disciple to the test, You hear My sayings and quote them, but do you do them—in your office, in your home life, in your private life? Notice the repulsion you feel toward anyone who tries to build with the sayings of Jesus. Our Lord allows no room for having some compartments holy and others unholy. Everything must be radically built on the foundation.

(d) Scriptural Concentration vv. 28–29

This summing up is a descriptive note by the Holy Spirit of the way in which the people who heard Jesus Christ were impressed by His doctrine. Its application for us is not, What would Jesus do? but, What did Jesus say? As we concentrate on what He said, we can stake our immortal souls upon His words. It is a question of scriptural concentration, not of sentimental consecration. When Jesus brings something home by His Word, don't shirk it. For example, something your brother has against you (see Matthew 5:23–24), some debt, something that presses—if you shirk that point, you become a religious humbug. The Holy Spirit's voice is as gentle as a zephyr, the merest check. When you hear it do you say, "But that is only a tiny detail, the Holy Spirit cannot mean that, it is much too trivial a thing"? The Holy Spirit does mean that, and at the risk of being thought fanatical you must obey.

When we are beginning to walk in the right way with God, we shall find the spirit of self-vindication will be unearthed; trying to fulfill what Jesus says will bring it to the light. What does it matter what anyone thinks of us as long as Jesus Christ thinks we are doing the right thing, as long as we can hear Him say, "Well done, good and faithful servant" (Matthew 25:21)?

NOTE TO THE READER

The publisher invites you to share your response to the message of this book by writing Discovery House Publishers, Box 3566, Grand Rapids, MI 49501, USA. For information about other Discovery House books, music, or videos, contact us at the same address or call 1-800-653-8333. Find us on the Internet at http://www.dhp.org/ or send E-mail to books@dhp.org.